NOMADS
OF THE WIND

INGO ARNDT / CLAUS-PETER LIECKFELD / PETER HUEMER

NOMADS

THE MIGRATION OF THE MONARCH BUTTERFLY

OF THE WIND

AND OTHER WONDERS OF THE BUTTERFLY WORLD

PAPADAKIS

When the prairie grass loses its color, monarch butterflies are about to begin the journey to their winter quarters in Mexico.

Aug.

"Birth"
Monarch 148

Sept.   Day 11

Oct.

Nov.

Dec.

Jan.

Feb.

Mar.

Apr.

A LATE SUMMER MORNING SOUTH OF THE GREAT LAKES

The morning the 11-day-old female monarch butterfly became the individual, *GJE 148*, began with a demonstration of freedom – purposeless freedom, to be exact. At first, the Indian Summer morning colored the ground fog a dusky pink, only to break up a blanket of myriad dew drops a short time later. The fog remained over Wolf Lake – located in the Richard Bong State Recreation Area, a few miles south of Milwaukee, Wisconsin – about one hour longer than in the surrounding area. There is no better way for a butterfly to be woken up: *148* felt the benefits of the warm, humid touch on her scaly body and knew... "Knew?"

We have already digressed. What do butterflies "know"? Surely knowledge is somewhat different for butterflies than it is for humans. Knowledge for the travel-ready monarchs could be something like an impulse, one that turns the wind into a wind of journey and then transforms the air into a conveyor belt that takes them over 2000 miles to the south-west – from the Great Lakes in the north-eastern United States to central Mexico. Perhaps it is a bodily urge to move forward? A drive to drive? Of course, all of that was only vaguely perceptible on this late summer morning. The young female monarch stretched her orange, black-veined wings toward the sun; a light following wind broke up the fog that danced on Wolf Lake – the eleventh day of life had started well. Or, at least, so it seemed.

On either side of the Burlington Road, which divides the recreation area, are sprawling fields of goldenrod – a veritable butterfly pasture. For *148* and those of her generation, it was a patch of paradise. And, on top of that, the small streams that ran north and south of the street endowed the air with just the right amount of moisture. But then *148* encountered a heavy gust of wind. Meanwhile, the cocoon in which she had spent the previous night was being

Aug.

"Birth"

Sept.
Monarch
148 is
decaled

Oct.

Nov.

Dec.

Jan.

Feb.

Mar.

Apr.

buffeted against a young sumac tree. With her round, faceted eyes, *148* could have seen that something threatening was coming her way – after all, butterflies can register fifteen times more individual movements per second than humans – but her attempt to flee landed her in a fine curtain of plastic threads.

Just a few minutes more warm-up time is all she would have needed that morning to achieve the proper body temperature for a quick start. But instead she had to endure being plucked from a net by a huge pair of tongs, in this case a human thumb and forefinger. All her legs, except the two front ones struggled frantically. Her antennae vibrated under the pull of her tense flight muscles. Nothing helped. The stress served to keep her from feeling the light pressure to her left wing case, to which a butterfly enthusiast attached a miniscule decal. On her wing, she now wore the code number *GJE 148*, given to her by the monarch research project of the University of Kansas, a project brought to life and overseen by Orley R. Taylor.

Taylor and his team are trying to solve one of the greatest mysteries of the animal kingdom: the migration of the monarch from the north-eastern United States and southern Canada to central Mexico – and back. The diminutive identity decals like the one *148* received are a key part of this research. The task also requires a great deal of both systematics and patience. We shall follow *148*, the feather-light emissary of science, on her flight – on the wings of scientifically controlled fantasy. And we shall also take the liberty of making any detours that may be necessary – what could perhaps be called explanatory holding patterns.

By mid-September the late summer winds have begun to cool. The native Indians, the Anishinabe who lived on the southern banks of the Great Lakes, used to say that you could taste the coming cold of winter on the tip of your tongue if you let the wind play on it during the warmth of late summer. On these banks, where the Anishinabe lived until their displacement, no one can do that any more. No human, anyway. But a flock of wading birds seem to have noticed that summer is waning. They set out from Green Bay, the 100-mile long north-west arm of Lake Michigan, flew southward along the western bank and took an inland turn to Wolf Lake. The lake and surrounding Richard Bong Recreation Area are traditional favorites of wading birds. The curved banks are also attractive to sandpipers, as well as the elegant white-breasted sprinters with their back plumage that resembles a brown shingle roof. One of the aforementioned *Tryngites subruficollis*, just recently fully mature, almost saw to it that the story of *148* finished before it had truly begun.

148 had just landed on a calyx when she registered a quick movement. The staccato images that flashed past her faceted eyes signaled: Flee, flee, flee! Too late! But, surprisingly, the sandpiper's beak missed her by a fraction. An eagle-eyed observer would probably have noticed that the buff-breasted sandpiper was nervous and hesitating as his scissor-like beak sped downward, just as a swordsman does when he lurches forward to attack, only to partially retreat and deflect because he has to parry a counter attack. The monarch's flaming orange-red colors had unnerved the bird. Her color and markings had sent him a trans-species message: "Be careful, poison!" Quite rightly as, like all monarchs *148* had made herself inedible by consuming poisonous milkweed in her previous life as a caterpillar.

It was not just *148*, but also the young sandpiper who was lucky on that September day. He saved

TAG@KU.EDU
MONARCH WATCH
1-888-TAGGING
GJE 148

himself a minute-long retching cramp. Chemists have given the name Cardenolides to the substances with which the monarch caterpillars impregnate their bodies by eating milkweed leaves. These are the substances bound to sugar molecules that are also found in foxgloves or on the skin of some toads. In order to keep from being easy prey, butterflies have developed trans-species preservation strategies. The German-born, Brazilian emigré Johan Friedrich Theodor Müller – whom Charles Darwin called "the Prince of Observers" – was the first to recognize that different species like to use the same, or very similar, "warning signs" to advertise their toxicity. In the nineteenth century, an Englishman Henry Walter Bates discovered that certain non-poisonous species in the South American rainforest used warning colors to trick their predators. They control this game of switch to their advantage: some brush-footed butterflies eschew the laborious task of poison storing and take on the warning colors of truly poisonous species closely related to the monarch. This "pretend-to-be-something-else," known as Batesian Mimicry, named after the man who discovered it, does not limit itself to markings, but also includes behavior: look-alikes even copy the flying styles of their archetypes. In fact, there was no obvious reason for *148* to leave the Richard Bong Recreation Area: she had food, warmth, pleasant winds that carried her from flower to flower and, just as importantly, there were relatively few butterfly hunters around. But *148* knew differently. She "knew" – as much as a lifeform with a miniscule brain can know – that she had to leave. Perhaps her antennae felt it or, perhaps, the sun flashed a signal. Here, we can only speculate. A number of days had passed since she received her number tag, and a couple more since she had her

ORLEY R. TAYLOR WANTS TO SOLVE ONE OF THE GREATEST MYSTERIES OF THE ANIMAL KINGDOM: THE MIGRATION OF THE MONARCH FROM THE NORTH-EASTERN UNITED STATES AND SOUTHERN CANADA TO CENTRAL MEXICO

Pages 12/13: *The latest monarch butterfly generation sets out on the journey south from the western banks of Lake Michigan.*

Pages 14/15: *They descend en masse on fields of flowers storing "fuel" for the energy-draining migration.*

Page 17: *The monarchs are decaled so that scientists can collect information on their flight path.*

Aug.

"Birth"

Sept.

Departure

Oct.

Nov.

Dec.

Jan.

Feb.

Mar.

Apr.

MONARCHS SOUTHBOUND

narrow escape from the sandpiper's beak. As September advanced she was clearly drawn south-westwards. At first she flew in circles that extended elliptically a little further to the south-west each day, but always ended with an about-turn to the banks of Wolf Lake. However, on September 17, her flight lost all vagueness, all approximation: *148* finally flew straight toward the south-west. The air was dry; high in the sky the sun unraveled a thin curtain of fair-weather clouds into single threads. The wind swirled aloft and carried her over the horizon. Far to the west, geese migrated southward in V-formation. North of Wood-stock, *148* met up with more monarchs, who had received the same call to depart. The majority of them had already traveled a good 300 miles – they had taken flight two days earlier from the Keweenaw Peninsula, which juts out into Lake Superior south of the renowned Isle Royale. The small, flaming orange flying brigade was spotted by a birdwatcher, an amateur ornithologist who had stopped at an artificially dammed stream to look for migratory birds. And he was right when he jotted in his birders' notebook: "monarchs southbound!"

Butterfly migration, and indeed all long-distance migration in general, was a puzzling phenomenon for quite some time and, in large part, still is today. The observation that many of the same butterflies were heading in the same direction at the same time was made long ago, but no rhyme nor reason for it could be determined. Perhaps the oldest, precise documentation about migrating white butterflies – probably the cabbage white on its way from Bavaria to Saxony – dates from 1100. About four hundred years later, Turpyn noted in his well-known *Chronicles of Calais: In the Reigns of Henry VII and Henry VIII* that butterflies are capable of flying over a strait, "On July 9, 1508, in the twenty-third year of Henry VII, on a Sunday, an enormous cloud of white butterflies flew over Calais, from north to south-east. It so resembled a heavy snowstorm, that at 4 o'clock in the afternoon, one could not even make out the city of Calais from St. Peter's church."

"There is no doubt," said the British founder of insect migration research, Carrington Bonsor Williams of this observation from the sixteenth century, "that they were talking about the large cabbage white butterfly – the time of year and the flight direction are in agreement with the reports [from the first decade of the twentieth century]." Exact observation and intelligent conclusions went mostly unnoticed before the invention of printing. But even later, when scientific observations could be read around the world, there was still disbelief. In the mid-nineteenth century, around 350 years after Turpyn's summer "snowstorm" in Calais, butterfly researcher E. Newman was forced to suffer the ill-tempered ridicule of his colleagues when he claimed to have made a similar observation at the same spot. It came to his attention that flocks of oleanders and blues fly over the English Channel – apparently deliberately and not just carried on the wind. At the time, no one believed that such a fragile creature was capable of such a feat. And when the ability of butterflies to travel great distances could finally no longer be called into question, the disbelief was reassigned to their ability to navigate. Carrington Bonsor Williams explained, "When the observation at sea irrefutably proved the astonishing flight performance, the disagreement about the existence of immigrant insect return flights began." The researchers – and not just insect researchers – had long forgotten the main imperative: let the facts speak! If this had not happened in the past, an obvious phenomenon would have been questioned by earlier generations of researchers: the

Pages 20/21: The Cape May peninsula, south of New York, is an important gathering place on the way to Mexico.

Pages 24/25: East of Cape May, the butterflies cross a large area of wetlands, which are bordered by important forage plants.

BUTTERFLIES ARE ABLE TO TRAVEL GREAT DISTANCES

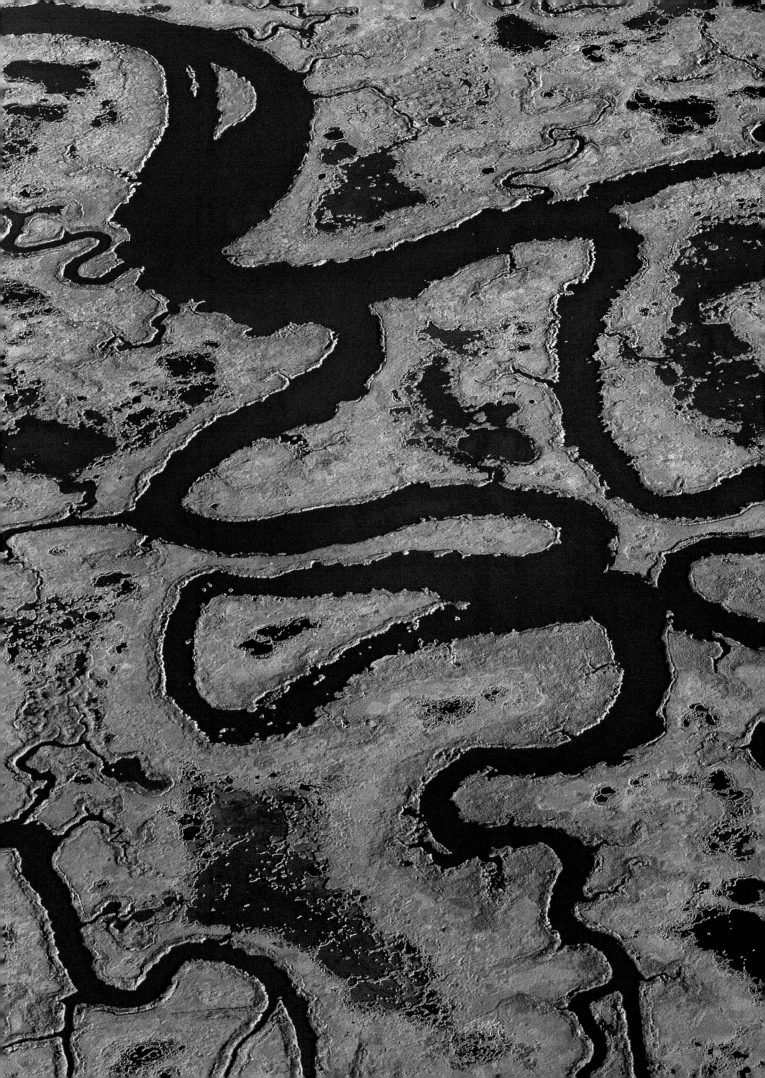

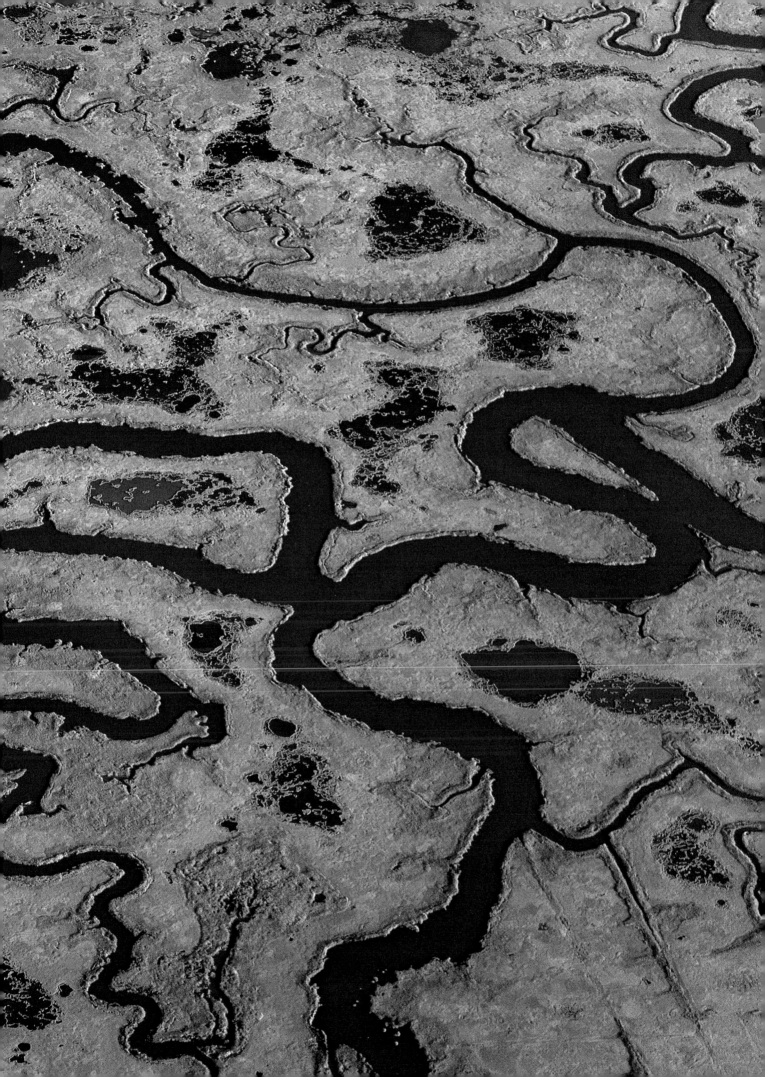

Aug.

"Birth"

Sept.

Quincy, Illinois
on the eastern
banks of the
Mississippi

Oct.

Nov.

Dec.

Jan.

GOLDENROD NECTAR IS THE BEST THING THAT CAN HAPPEN TO A MONARCH BUTTERFLY

Feb.

Mar.

Apr.

Opposite and pages 28/29:
*Goldenrod flowers have a magical
appeal. Their nectar is a favorite
meal for the large, migrating
butterflies.*

congregation of monarchs at Cape May, the exposed southern tip of New Jersey's coastline, which – unlike *148* and the monarchs that depart from the western Great Lakes – fly along part of the Atlantic coast in a southerly direction before turning inland toward central Mexico. Presumably the 12-mile-wide opening of Delaware Bay causes the migrating butterflies to hesitate briefly – just long enough to highlight a few remarkable days in autumn with the color orange. This hesitation is the result of conflicting impulses: on one hand, there is the urge to fly the preset direction, on the other a warning, "Be careful, dangerously large body of water ahead!" And it is not until the urge to head south kicks in that the warning can be ignored and the water negotiated. It is then that those out walking can see small flying brigades set out toward the sea. How do they know that they will reach land after flying for twelve miles?

The longstanding doubt about the performance of species that travel great distances is understandable, For a long time, there have been many wrong ideas or misconceptions about the life expectancy of the adults – the so-called "imagines" – of many insect species. For example, the fact that the brimstone butterfly – a flashy and not unusual representative of its genus – can live for ten to eleven months was not known for a very long time. On the other hand, it was known that butterflies often depend on a very specific nectar diet, nectar that is not always available on a long journey. The availability of suitable nectar "filling stations" is one of the smaller problems *148* will encounter on her 2000-mile journey southward because the butterfly, unlike the caterpillar that it once was, is not limited to a single plant species. A butterfly takes any nourishment it can find that is suitable, available, and accessible without too much effort. Flowering

plants with specific chemical compounds – pyrrolizidine alkaloids – are the favorite; plants of the daisy family offer both quality and quantity.

A few miles north of Quincy, Illinois, on the eastern banks of the Mississippi, *148* encounters her first heavy turbulence. A thundercloud looks as though it will flatten such a feather-light flyer as the storm passes over. However, we have to believe that a creature equipped with an almost inconceivable long-distance flight program is also programmed with strong wind navigation and avoidance capabilities. The Midwest is a challenge. It is flat and burned out from the all too hot summer. Field after field of inedible plants stretching to the horizon constitute a long distance without food for *148*. If

these butterfly wastelands become too desolate, even a long-distance traveler – who is, by nature, able to withstand suffering – would perish at some point. But just able to survive is to be alive: weakened by days of flying without nourishment, *148* stumbles, a few miles west of Parsons, Kansas, onto a vast field of goldenrod. Along a former cattle path, worn flat by decades of use, this member of the daisy family raises its golden yellow, curved panicle racemes toward the sky. Goldenrod nectar is one of the best things that can happen to a monarch butterfly; and for a long-distance migrant, who has already (if one compares her with a human long distance runner) flown for a very long distance in an anaerobic state, goldenrod must be as good as nourishing food and a pick-me-up all in one.

Aug.

"Birth"

Sept.

Oct.

Nov. Guadalupe
      Mountains

Dec.

Jan.

Feb.

Mar.

Apr.

On November 1, when she was well over 1200 miles from her birthplace in Wisconsin, *148* reached southwestern Texas. In the Guadalupe Mountains, she was carried on the updraft, drifting seemingly aimlessly in the hot air of the semi-desert. But this was deceptive. The south-facing mountain range channeled the airflow in just the right direction. *148* flew through one of the most beautiful parts of the United States – with a handful of fellow travelers at first, but then they took a different route at Upper Dog Canyon. On November 3 she reached El Capitán, a craggy, imperious, unapproachable limestone formation at the south-east edge of the Guadalupe Mountains National Park. This majestic rock mass once reared up as a reef in the waters of an age-old inland sea long before either humans or butterflies existed. About twelve thousand years ago, early humans roamed these lands hunting mammoths. Even then, shortly after the Ice Age, the climate here was humid. Is it possible that monarchs were on the move in prehistoric times?

Recent studies show that the southern monarch, which is very similar to the long-distance migrant of today, split off from a common ancestor about two million years ago. That may sound like a long time, but if you take into consideration how many years butterflies have existed on earth, it is just a wing flutter away from today. The oldest American butterfly fossils – *Praepapilio colorado, Praepapilio gracilis* and *Riodinella nympha* – are from the Eocene epoch. The 48-million-year-old fossils were found in the shale of the Green River Formation in Colorado. A skipper butterfly fossil found in recent years in Denmark is even a few million years older than that, dating from the Paleocene epoch, about 55 million years ago. And probably the oldest moth fossil was found in the Blue Lias Formations – lower Jurassic – in Dorset, England. It is almost 200 million years old. If England, the home of paleontology,

was not the home of the first bird, Achaeopteryx – that was the Bavarian Altmühl valley region – it is at least the location where another atavistic flyer was found: *Archeolepis mane*. Clearly verifiable evidence is rare – a butterfly or moth seldom leaves any traces or imprints for posterity – but we can assume that, with the evolution of flowering plants in the Cretaceous period (which began 135 million years ago and ended about 65 million years ago), there was a rapid rise in the number of butterflies and moths. Whether or not these primitive, fluttering creatures undertook extensive migrations at that time still cannot be clarified, even with the refined research techniques of today.

At the point where Guadalupe Canyon separates from the National Park, *148* rejoins the group she lost at Upper Dog Canyon. The troop has been decimated. One is missing a third of its rear left wing, a loss that does not impair flight capability – or, not to the extent that it can be detected by the human eye. Underneath a long, overhanging cliff, the flying brigade is drawn by something that can be considered a performance-enhancing additive to their regular nourishment of flower nectar. The rocky projection exudes moisture that drips and forms a shallow puddle beneath. The monarchs all dip their proboscises into this "mineral water." As they drink, a hot surface wind makes their wings quiver. After a few minutes, the migration break is over – an orange cloud swirls up and away.

"Migration" is not something that can be defined in one breath – not as it pertains to butterflies. Science distinguishes different categories of migrating butterflies and moths: seasonal migrants, inland migrants and area expanders. In addition, there is a fourth category for all migrating species about which nothing concrete is yet known. Such seasonal migrants as the painted lady butterfly and the convolvulus hawk moth leave their original homelands annually and fly to other areas to reproduce. The new generation flies back to the parental homeland. In the special case of the monarch, the return journey requires several generations. Some species only leave their birthplace in order to spend part of the year in a more favorable location. Egg deposition then takes place back in the original homeland. Unlike *homo sapiens*, butterflies and moths reproduce during the last stage of their life. Most inland migrants, as the name suggests, migrate only within their area of circulation. But some fly beyond it, and reach habitats not suitable for long-term colonization. They, and their offspring, die in the foreign location – a one-way flight, so to speak. The area expanders are more successful. They manage to settle in areas never before colonized. They are pioneers, new territory settlers, inland migrants that settle in new terrain far from their original homeland. A prime example of this is the humming-bird hawk moth. Global warming at the end of the twentieth century enabled it to extend its territory and it now populates a region north of the Alps. We humans are responsible for an additional, fifth category – we shall call it the forced migrant. People displace species – sometimes on purpose, usually unwittingly. And this is how the horse chestnut leaf miner was brought into Austria in the mid 1980s. Within two decades, the moth spread throughout Europe and causes much dismay when it browns the leaves of horse chestnuts in summer. This unprecedented, successful moth relocation, was presumably made possible by a change in the host plant. There is evidence that the miner moth switched its diet from maple leaf to horse chestnut and, in so doing, was able to get rid of its enemies: ichneumonids (or ichneumonid wasps), which use a

Pages 30/31: *As they fly over the hot, arid areas of the US southern states, the butterflies continually land to drink.*

IN THE GUADALUPE MOUNTAINS, SHE WAS CARRIED ON THE UPDRAFT, DRIFTING SEEMINGLY AIMLESSLY IN THE HOT AIR OF THE SEMI-DESERT

stinger to inject butterfly and moth eggs, caterpillars or pupae with their eggs, and in so doing kill them. But ichneumonids, the parasites of miner moths, do not like horse chestnut – yet.

El Capitán, a legendary, towering sheer cliff of red limestone was a couple of flight hours behind *148* and the others and they had drifted a number of miles south of Guadalupe Canyon when they suddenly encountered a sandstorm. A howling gale swept over the tiny grains of the pulverized earth and hit them with thousands of tiny bullets. Within a few seconds, the migrating group was driven apart. *148* collapsed her wings vertically over her body and let herself fall. Once on the canyon floor, she gyrated with her strong legs as quickly as she could and thus managed to escape the sand and find protection from the wind. The luminous white spots in the black edges of her forewings were almost gray with dust when she finally found shelter. She forced herself into a hollow between pebbles that had been ground smooth by a flood over a thousand years ago. A mouse – normally an enemy of the monarch despite the butterfly's toxicity – scurried by dangerously close, but it was obviously not on the hunt but in search of a reliable windshield. Few mouse species eat monarchs that are on the ground. The black-eared mouse is a specialized monarch hunter and thus has enormous feeding reserves almost all to itself.

Although she had succeeded in avoiding the immediate danger, *148* still had many difficulties to confront. The sandstorm lasted for three days, three days in which the long-distance migrant remained motionless and could not procure food. Like all butterflies, monarchs can fast. But this fast came at a bad time. The tiny creature had been forced into maximum performance and its associated

LESS THAN 600 MILES TO GO

Pages 34/35: *The Guadalupe Mountains rise from the earth in southern Texas. At sunset, the craggy rock faces of El Capitán glow in warm red tones.*

Page 36: *From the Guadalupe Mountains National Park it is only a few miles to Mexico.*

To take photographs from the air, Ingo Arndt flew over the monarch butterfly colonies in an ultra-light plane.

energy use. Worse still, *148* was nearing the Guadalupe National Park border. More fasting would rob her of the energy she needed to continue her journey. Very soon she would sense, not realize, her options: either search for nectar among the granular rubble and risk being pelted with debris in the process, or become completely devitalized and die.

At the end of the third day, the low-lying sun bathed the southern Guadalupe Canyon and the Delaware mountains bordering it to the east in a magical red light. The wind fell. First it was less strong and then, little by little, it abated considerably. Finally it was too weak to blow the sand through the air. It simply swished through the yucca palms and tugged lightly at the pinyon-juniper. Small falcons were the first to soar up into the air. They seemed to know that a multitude of hungry little creatures would be

THEY CAN DO IT. MILLIONS OF THEM PROVE IT EVERY YEAR

coming out of hiding – hastily, ravenously and, therefore, carelessly. *148*, too, arose and lurched forward, in a southerly direction. The glowing red center of a purple coneflower signaled rescue. To be honest, we do not know – or, at least we do not know with any certainty – how butterflies perceive bright red. We do know, though, that butterfly eyes are among the most multifaceted in the animal kingdom. They range from the large, compound eyes of the butterfly to the simple eyes of the caterpillar. The males of one unusual butterfly group even have optical organs in a place humans would never think of: on their genitals. With the aid of these photoreceptors, they can control copulation and precisely position their sexual organs.

Another special butterfly capability is, perhaps, more familiar. Ultraviolet light receptors allow diurnal species to detect flower patterns, and therefore important food signals that we cannot see. This means that, for butterflies, a flower that appears to us as monochrome, has on it a kind of "landing strip" that magically attracts them. Similarly, the ultraviolet light receptors play a role in the search of many butterflies for a partner. A large number of butterflies carry "flares" that – as we are unable to discern anything in the ultraviolet spectrum with the naked eye – we cannot detect. Step-by-step, scientists are delving into the world of butterfly perceptions. They discovered a while ago that for some moths – of whom it was long said that they locate flowers exclusively with their sense of smell – starlight is sufficient to recognize the color of important flowers. This means that they see multi-colored images in places where we might just be able to make out the difference between almost black and black itself.

A few flight hours after the lifesaving coneflower meal in Fort Hancock, Texas, home of the old Camp Rice, *148* flew 600 feet above the wide band of the Rio Grande. She floated, as only a butterfly can, over the Texas/Mexico border. And if this border crossing were part of a road movie, the soundtrack would have to segue from US country and western to Mexican folk music, with its artistic guitar runs and trumpet solos. Head up, *148*. Antennae to the wind. Breast muscle flexed. Less than 600 miles to go!

They can do it. Millions of them prove it every year: The great transcontinental flight begins somewhere in the Great Lakes region and ends in central Mexico, on the Transvolcanic Mountains of Michoacán. Like clockwork. How in the world is this possible? Dr. Taylor from the Monarch Research Project at the University of Kansas – who is responsible for the decal *148* has carried with her for many hundreds of flight hours already – first suspected that the sun plays a part in the great orientation puzzle. He shipped monarchs that would have headed south from Kansas to Washington, DC, on the east coast of the United States. Every specimen he set free there, without the slightest time delay, headed south, as though the shipping had not taken place. They flew on a course that would have taken them to the Florida peninsula, not central Mexico. (Monarchs, incidentally, also overwinter in Florida.) But science has not yet come to understand if, or how, they integrate themselves into the seasonal, trans-continental air traffic. As soon as Dr. Taylor had captured the test flyers he had shipped to the east coast and held them behind a fly screen for a few days – he did this so that they could experience the sunrise and sunset – they orientated themselves anew. And they did it correctly! They chose a course that allowed them to aim toward their original destination. The only logical explanation: the sun led the way. Can it be that the *Danaus plexippus* calculates the angle of radiation and latitude based on the sunrise and sunset? And if so, how does such

data translate into a reliable travel guide? But the sunlight experiment did not prove that that there was not something else, such as the earth's magnetic field, that played a role. In fact, science did uncover the key significance of the magnetic field line. Autumnally migrating monarchs were tested under three conditions: they were subjected to normal conditions; then to an artificially reversed magnetic field; and, finally, to a total block of all magnetic influences. The results were absolutely clearcut: in the natural conditions they would normally en-counter, the migrating monarchs did what they always do – they flew south. With the artificial reversal of the magnetic field they did the opposite and flew towards the north-east. And when all magnetic influences were blocked, the monarchs became completely disoriented. The results of these two experiments indicate a dual guidance system.

This would be extraordinary but not unimaginable. We know from the research into bird migration that long-distance travelers can, if necessary, "change channels" from magnetic field to celestial bodies for guidance. Birds, after all, have a brain even if it is only a tiny mini-computer the size of a hazelnut. Butterflies, on the other hand, have only a quasi brain at their disposal – entomologists speak of a "rope-ladder nervous system." This is an elongated organ, found roughly where the spine of a vertebrate is located. Monarchs are obviously able to achieve without a high-class brain some things that those with superbrains cannot. Perhaps we should question our classification system. In evaluating insects,we tend to be rather mammal centered. Categorization into higher and lower life forms may consistently lead us astray when we are assessing insect life. An eighteenth-century pioneer of insect research, René-Antoine Ferchault de Réaumur, placed insects at the top of the natural order – and, what is more, he did this at a time

when the evaluation of "vermin" was still considered blasphemous and, therefore, dangerous. According to Réaumur, the body structure of insects had more character and greatness than the movements of the planets, which, he said, were nothing more than "a game played with orbs."

In mid-November, *148* reached her destination: the mountainside of the Mexican Michoacán highlands, near the small town of Angangueno. The chapped, brown surface of the mountains stretches to the horizon. Colonies of lumberjacks have robbed the land of its forest covering, ripping out the trees with axes and chainsaws – but they have not managed to reach the peaks. Against the parched grassy meadows and small fields rise the rich green canopies of the Oyamel firs. Fortunately, many of them are still inaccessible to lumber trucks.

Those arriving at this dot on the map in winter are confronted by an even bigger monarch butterfly puzzle. Why do millions and millions of these long-distance migrants gather in winter almost exclusively on the branches of the Oyamel firs? Do the conifers emit some irresistible substance or something vital to their survival? To the human nose, the mountain forests – which grow up to 10,000 feet above sea level – simply smell like Mediterranean pine forests: earthy, strong, aromatic. Perhaps the bark offers the monarchs a unique microclimate so perfect that it is worth a 2000-mile journey.

Anyone seeing the thick layer of dead butterflies under the branches cannot but doubt this. So many victims! In mid-January, 1992, 90 per cent of one of the largest colonies, at more than 10,000 feet, was wiped out by a single cold front as it swept through. Moisture and rapid cooling delivered a deadly double blow. The periodically recurring mass deaths were examined in detail. Studies showed

Pages 40/41: *The branches of the Oyamel fir, the predominant winter quarters, are covered with luminous butterflies.*

Pages 42/43: *Many millions of these creatures overwinter in a single colony. The fir branches are completely covered in butterflies.*

Page 44: *In the middle of the day, life in the colony literally explodes.*

Pages 46/47: *The suction created by warm air rising sends the monarch butterflies reeling.*

Right: *Huge numbers of warmth-hungry winter visitors collect in sunny spots.*

Aug.

"Birth"

Sept.

Oct.

Nov.

Arrival in the winter quarters in Mexico

Dec.

Jan.

Feb.

Mar.

Apr.

that mass death occurred when extreme cold and dampness came together. The forest floor underneath the conifers was a sea of orange-red. In January 2002, a research team examined storm damage in monarch colonies. They found that the surviving butterflies from the denser colonies – those in which about three-quarters of the winter visitors had been killed by a single, heavy January storm – usually relocated a few hundred yards from the site of the catastrophe, as if wishing to distance themselves from the scene of death. Presumably, the survivors are obeying an inherited piece of evolutionary wisdom by avoiding the inevitable pathogenic bacteria formed by the decomposition of many millions of their fellow monarchs.

In view of such enormous losses, the cost/efficiency question simply cannot be overlooked: surely winter quarters should be less hazardous and, above all, warmer? Is a winter at more than 10,000 feet above sea level, where there are occasional snow storms and periodically recurring, dangerously cold moisture, so much more favorable than a winter on the southern edge of the Great Lakes along the border of the United States and Canada? There must be a reason for the trip to Mexico, one that humans have not yet uncovered, a reason that carries more weight than the millions of butterfly lives lost. Experts estimate that in the winter of 2002 the number of overwintering monarchs was a meager 28 million. They believe that twice to four times that number would be normal.

The story of monarch research is still young. On January 2, 1975, husband and wife scientists Cathy and Ken Bugger came across the Mexican winter colony. To call them the "discoverers" would be to deny history because, of course, the native population had been aware of the winter "hotels"

THE BRANCHES OF THE TREES BECOME RUST-RED

for centuries. But when they saw the huge concentration of monarchs – which had been proposed as "the official national insect of the USA" – they realized they were dealing with a species that, in the most extraordinary circumstances, had flown diagonally across half the North American continent.

The first weeks in *148*'s Mexican quarters are cold but, luckily, not particularly wet. She has gone from individual butterfly to being part of a vibrant superorganism – a gigantic insect with millions of wings. When the cold bites, a blanket of fellow monarchs keeps *148* warm – the branches of the trees are now rust-red. White-winged troopial, birds the size of finches, descend on the agglomeration. They have devised a paring technique that allows them to open up the parts of the monarch that are particularly nutritious. Whenever the birds attach themselves to a branch, hundreds of butterflies in the vicinity flutter to the ground, as if they are reacting to an inaudible warning cry. Under the midday sun, more and more individuals open their wings and, sometimes – even when no enemy is around – an entire segment, some comprising anywhere from a hundred to a thousand butterflies, fly off to drink or find nectar. As in the case of flocks of starlings and gaggles of geese, not one of them gives a signal to depart, and yet there must have been a signal or impulse of some sort.

One day *148* was pulled down by a large cluster of hundreds of butterflies. Before she could open her wings – it was colder than the normal operational flight temperature – she was swept under many layers of half-stiff comrades. Normally, it would have been enough for *148* to hold tight for a while until the sun engendered sufficient warmth. It should have been just a few minutes before the butterflies became a flying carpet once more. But on this occasion, something hard rushed through

the red-brown sea of wings. Ramos, the nine-year-old son of a peasant, from a nameless tract of three-family homes just north of Angangueo, was on a treasure hunt. A monarch wing with a signature would net him and his family five dollars. FIVE DOLLARS if he could tell the gringo who came at the end of the month exactly where he had found the butterfly with the numbered decal. His father had to work many hours building roads for three dollars. The road on which he labours many days a year will lead to the vicinity of the butterfly forests. And it is wide enough for lumber trucks. That could mean that the illegal deforestation of the "butterfly trees" – in 1986, the Mexican government placed the monarch wintering areas under protection – could become yet more extensive. The danger to Mexico's largest natural wonder has been recognized and the sanctuary significantly enlarged by about 60,000 hectares. But the lumberjacks are not impressed.

Counter pressure can come only from the locals themselves, from those who profit from the annual butterfly tourism: hotel operators, drivers, nature guides, small restaurant owners. Often even the concerned, ecologically-friendly tourist does not realize that the wood used to prepare his black beans and spicy sausage is from trees that have been cut down in the forest he has traveled so far to see. All in all, there is hope that one of the natural wonders of the world will be better protected from illegal tree felling. Local nature guides are being trained, and it is hoped that the proceeds from entrance fees to especially attractive parts of the sanctuary will not flow into dark channels where they trickle away before they can benefit the lives of the local people.

Ramos knows nothing about all these confusing confrontations: lumberjacks versus tourist-oriented

"Birth"

Sept.

Oct.

Nov.

Dec.

Jan.

Feb.

Winter
quarters
in Mexico

Page 50: *After a cold night in the highlands, many of the butterflies sit in the midday sun with open wings or go in search of nourishment.*

Pages 52/53: *A ray of sun breaks through the thick, mountain forest and shines a spotlight on a monarch in flight.*

Pages 54-57: *During longer dry spells, the monarch butterflies search for the last remaining water sources. Some face the threat of drowning when they get caught up in the mad rush to drink.*

Page 59: *The mountain forests in the Mexican highlands are dwindling because of illegal deforestation. The monarch butterfly suffers casualties as a result.*

users and local, traditional impact/rights of use versus species conservation. He is only concerned with what is in it for him. Last winter he found five wings. No child of his age found more. At school, the teacher explained that the gringos wanted to know how a *mariposa monarcha*, which travels right across the United States and finds its way to Mexico. The more decals Ramos and his friends can discover, the easier it will be for researchers to find an answer – or something like that.

Why are gringos so interested in the butterflies, Ramos wanted to know. But the Angangueo grade school teacher said only that it was an interesting question and that perhaps Ramos could ask Eduardo Rendón Salinas. Everyone in Angangueo knows Eduardo. When he is not on the road with Lincoln P. Brower and his research group, or with other international monarch experts, he oversees the reforestation of the bare mountainsides with the Oyamel fir, for WWF-México. But on his way to Eduardo – the locals knew exactly where to find him on this cold February day – Ramos came across a congregation of monarchs around a puddle. A lot of drinking *mariposa* can be seen on dry days. And this day was so dry, that breathing in the thin mountain air burned the nostrils. Ramos left the puddle alone – to look for decaled monarchs among live ones would be a wasted effort because it would only set red sparks flying, like a fire when dry twigs are added. Farther up the mountain, Ramos finds a thick layer of motionless monarchs spread out under the trees and particularly close together. What an opportunity! He could find and question Eduardo Rendón Salinas tomorrow, thought Ramos, perhaps today was his lucky day. But no, today Ramos's luck was bad – bad because the luck was just within his reach but then literally fluttered away. A decaled butterfly flew up from the layer of moving butterflies and just escaped the child's grasping hand – it was an even narrower escape than the one from the sandpiper many weeks ago at Wolf Lake.

148 felt the push of a fingertip, spun on her own axis and let herself be swept away with her comrades as they flew off. She had very nearly become a victim of the cold and its laming effect on flight capability. Both cold and heat present major challenges for butterflies – the body temperature of poikilotherms corresponds directly with the outdoor temperature. And that is not always butterfly friendly. Heat seems to be a lesser problem. Butterflies can effectively protect themselves from overheating with the

WHY ARE GRINGOS SO INTERESTED IN THE BUTTERFLIES, RAMOS WANTED TO KNOW

Aug.

"Birth"

Sept.

Oct.

Nov.

Dec.

Jan.

Feb.   Winter
        quarters
        in Mexico

Mar.

Apr.

airstream they create. If that does not work, they sometimes crawl to a shady spot. Some species can also shift the overheated bodily fluids of the breast – which is well insulated against the cold – to the less insulated abdomen. It has even been established that there are some species of moth that cool down by regurgitating fluid – cooling by evaporation! As a rule, cold – or more correctly, relative cold – is a bigger problem. A dark color, which perfectly absorbs the sunlight is a tried and tested method in the struggle for existence. Some species attract attention with their thick, protective body hair. Others extend the developmental phases – egg, caterpillar, pupa, butterfly – for an astonishingly long time period. The pupal stage of the alpine eggar moth, *Eriogaster arbusculae*, can last for seven years to allow acclimatization to the harsh spring of the Alps and Scandinavia. The egg clutches are programmed so that only some of the moths hatch each year, thus keeping down the number of casualties during cold snaps. However, what is not programmable is the "human" catastrophe factor. The long pupal stage makes adolescent alpine eggar moths near ground level vulnerable to radioactivity. The effects of the reactor accident in Chernobyl annihilated the species in many areas. Experts always have to search if they want to find butterfly parents caring for the brood in the wild: *Eriogaster arbusculae* mothers protect their eggs from the cold with "wool" plucked from their own bodies. Protection from the cold often requires extremely radical solutions: in regions where there are high, sustained winds, such as Tierra del Fuego, and also at high altitudes, the conditions that make it difficult for moths to reach the proper flight temperature. Countless species have abandoned their wings. This is particularly true of females, because they do not need to fly to mate and can simply wait to be

There is hope that the monarch butterfly's winter quarters will be preserved. Nature preservation organizations have begun a reforestation program on the bare mountains.

Page 62/63: In the central highlands of Mexico, there remain only a few cohesive areas of forest lined with old trees, the ones the monarchs need.

WWF-MEXICO IS OVERSEEING REFORESTATION OF THE BARE MOUNTAINS, WITH THE OYAMEL FIR

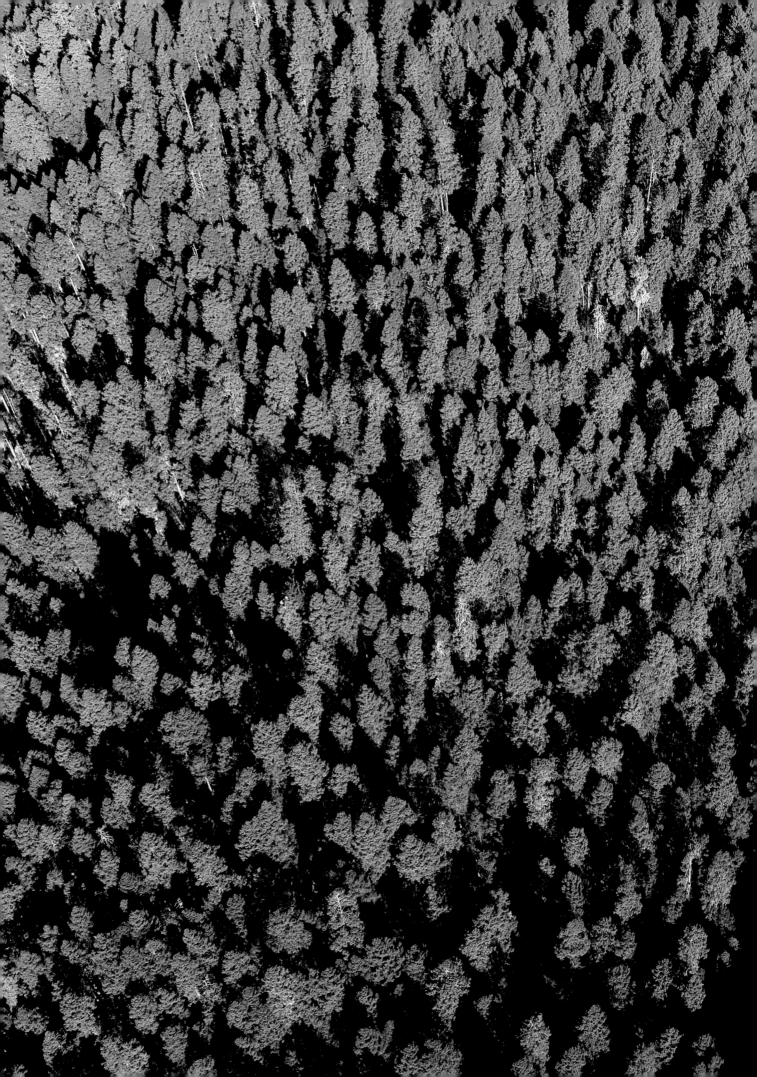

sought and found. The obvious advantage of this radical solution is two-pronged: less energy consumption and a defense against drifting away on the wind. On sub-Antarctic islands, in extreme cases both genders move about without wings as do females of some species in the Alps – by hopping forward. It seems as if evolution may perhaps be preparing to reinvent the grass-hopper principle.

Basically, butterflies can control their activities by basking in the sunshine. Amazingly, they assume a reflective crouch by positioning themselves with a half-open V-wing toward the sun, so that the rays are reflected from one forewing to the other and even onto the body. Another technique, one also used by humans, albeit more unfavorably than favorably, is that when it is really cold they shiver.

BUTTERFLIES POSITION THEMSELVES WITH A HALF-OPEN V-WING TOWARD THE SUN, SO THAT THE RAYS ARE REFLECTED FROM ONE FOREWING TO THE OTHER AND EVEN ONTO THE BODY

As the sun sets, more light penetrates the dark mountain forest. The monarchs make full use of every opportunity for sunbathing.

Depending on the species, many butterflies and moths need operational temperatures, or, to be exact, inner body temperatures, to be between 34° and 43° Celsius. We know that the species active in high temperatures can exist only in the tropics. Here, the conditions are optimal, and the large number of species is no surprise. Butterflies and moths in temperate or even northern latitudes must be, more or less, able to handle the cold weather. So what does a moth do when temperatures in the high mountains – or during the late fall – drop to between 0° and 10° Celsius? The few males that are still out and about lower their wing beat rates to a mere four per second and can thus be said to have invented a new cold flight technique. For butterflies how cold it is is not the only pertinent question. Rather more important seems to be: *When* is it cold? The majority of butterfly and moth species in the caterpillar stage outlive the hard

Aug.

"Birth"

Sept.

Oct.

Nov.

Dec.

Jan.

Feb.

Winter
quarters
in Mexico

Mar.

Apr.

winter in the northern hemisphere. This is presumably because caterpillars can burrow underground or retreat into sheltered hiding places, whereas the immobile pupa or eggs must persevere wherever they are. Relatively few species – but including the peacock and the small tortoiseshell – overwinter as adults, as butterflies or moths, in hiding places that offer adequate protection from the cold.

The moist, cold air at the end of February was both a threat and an opportunity for *148*. The cold left many thousands of her fellow monarchs dead, dropping to the ground like autumn leaves or dead flower petals. But the humidity also has its good side: it encourages mountain flowers to sprout. *148* had a long drink and lots of nectar. Her proboscis once more proved itself to be the perfect eating/drinking utensil. Before a precision landing on a flower, she had already unrolled this flexible drinking straw. And, in order to make the nectar search a single uninterrupted movement, she refrained from rolling back her proboscis after each stop. Just how nature came up with the proboscis, the insect proboscis in particular, has been described as follows: the proboscis was necessary. Another question posed during the Cretaceous period was: what do pollinators need to ensure that the job is done successfully?

The proboscis was an ingenious half-answer. The proboscis of the "modern" butterfly and moth comprises two tiny, half-tube-like hoses, which are folded into each other in a most complex way. Imagine two drinking straws sliced down the center lengthwise and then pushed in and over each other to make a single straw – albeit one that also has the same quality as the party-poppers that are so popular at children's birthday parties and New Year's Eve celebrations.

HOW NATURE CAME UP WITH THE PROBOSCIS

Even in their winter quarters, monarchs need nourishment. Their long proboscis allows them to suck the nectar from the calyxes of flowers.

The complicated roll out/roll in mechanism of the butterfly and moth proboscis was, for a long time, an object of constant bickering among experts. It is only recently that we are sure that it is the pressure of the hemolymph – insect blood – that rolls out the proboscis, while the muscles used to create feeding suction roll it back in. These muscles also provide the strong suction needed to pull the nectar and water through the tube and into the digestive system. Moth proboscises can be impressively long. The European convolvulus hawk moth works with a 4-inch-long tube, while its tropical relatives can, in extreme cases, extend it to 11 inches. Such representatives as these often have the monopoly on flowers with long calyxes, flowers that could never be pollinated without these specialists. A long calyx on the one hand, and a long proboscis on the other is a classic case of the co-evolution of plant and insect. The principle functions on the basis of each one benefiting the other: the flower can be pollinated despite its long, narrow calyx, which in turn ensures that a host of uninvited guests are not able to penetrate it; and the moth acquires an exclusive, competition-free food source. The partners do, however, take a considerable risk: the absence of one of them constitutes a death sentence for its partner.

On cold, cloudy winter days the colony is quiet. The butterflies hang motionless in the fir trees.

Pages 70/71: A sudden cold front can kill a large part of a colony within a few hours. The forest floor is then covered with a deep layer of dead butterflies.

THE COLD LEFT MANY THOUSANDS OF HER FELLOW MONARCHS DEAD AND FALLING TO THE GROUND LIKE AUTUMN LEAVES

For *148* , every ounce of energy is now vital. With the coming spring, her life is nearing its final quarter and, yet, a series of important events still lies before her: finding a partner, mating, taking off in a north-easterly direction (toward the Great Lakes), and laying her eggs. By mid-March, the Oyamel branches have begun to shed their colorful decorations just as deciduous trees shed their leaves. Fewer and fewer monarchs return to their tree branches after a day

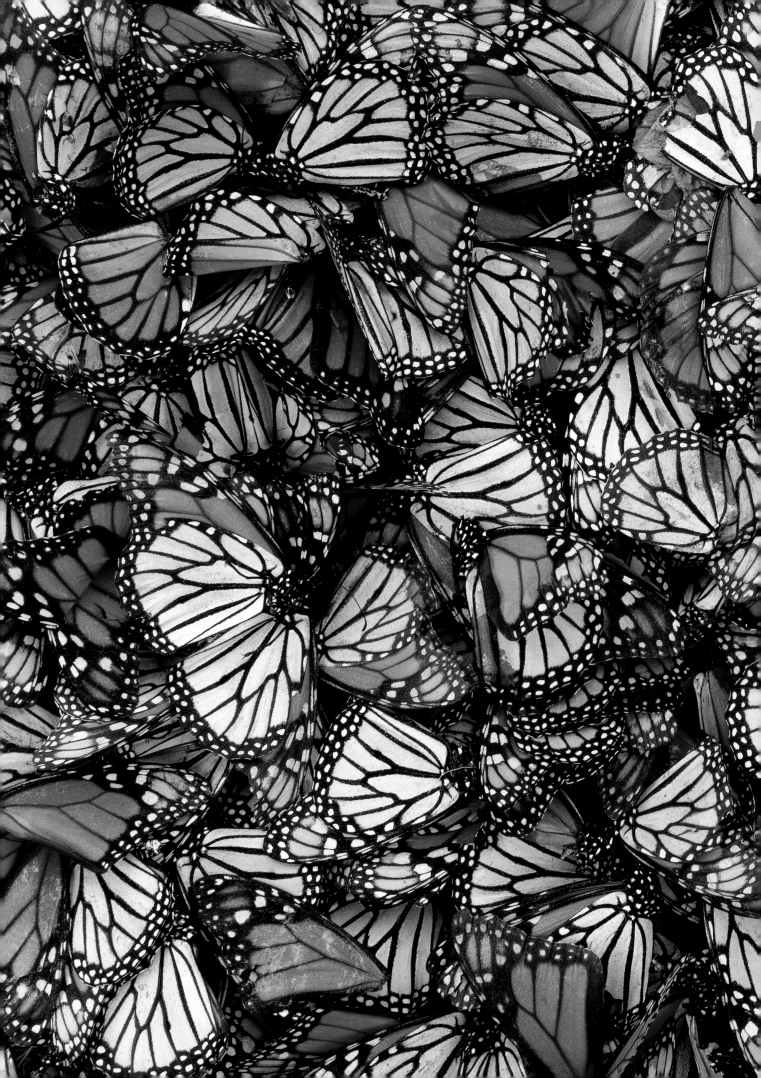

Aug.

"Birth"

Sept.

Oct.

Nov.

Dec.

Jan.

Feb.

Mar.

Prior to
return
flight

Apr.

out in the ever-warmer sunshine. And those heading north early are well advised. The day before *148*'s long return trip, cold rain falls and freezes to form a thin layer of ice as it hits the ground. Late frost! During the preceding days, steady following winds from the Pacific had induced the rain-heavy clouds to unload their cargo over the foothills. But as the wind lost its energy the moisture-filled clouds rose up over the monarch region and mass casualties became a real threat. Many members of the colony had fallen from the fir boughs like a pile of lifeless flakes. *148* lay, stunned, under a blanket of bodies. But the next day, when the strong sun suddenly took control again, the thousands of bodies covering *148* warmed up. She struggled and escaped. Time to go – high time!

If, more than a half year ago, an eternity for a monarch, *148* felt the urge to fly in a south-westerly direction from Wolf Lake on the western banks of Lake Michigan right across the south-western states to Mexico, now she experienced the pull of the north-east. We do not know on what part of the butterfly's body this pull is exerted. Parallel to the profound urge to travel, something else is stirring inside that tiny body, something that sharpens the sense of smell and sends light tremors over the forewings like a fine vibrato. There is something in the air. Something that we humans can only inadequately describe – and even less adequately pinpoint – as "spring fever."

Monarchs smell what attracts them most: sex and food. Their antennae are studded with thousands of tiny, raised sense receptors– and a number of recessed ones as well. Certain moths, such as the silk moth, have about 17,000 olfactory cilia. These are also found in other places on the body, in the area of the labial palps, although these do not play

TIME TO GO –
HIGH TIME

The frequent sunny weather in the Michoacán mountain forests is often interrupted by periods of inclement weather. After a heavy rain shower, a monarch butterfly drinks the raindrops dotted over its body.

Aug.

"Birth"

Sept.

Oct.

Nov.

Dec.

Jan.

Feb.

Mar.

Mating

Apr.

anywhere near the same role as the antennae receptors. Adult butterflies and moths need their many thousands of "antennae noses" for use in three areas of life: to find food, to find plants on which to deposit their eggs and for their offspring, and to find partners with whom to breed. The most exciting and wonderful, of course, are the sexual scents. Finding partners and copulation are almost always scent-driven, say the experts, who have a name for the messenger substance: sexual pheromones. The males as well as the females can exude very special scents. Some males have the capability of locating the female scent from a distance of several miles. The male scent is very different. Think of it is as an aphrodisiac – male beguiles female – as the mood maker for copulation. But the male butterfly quickly puts the brakes on this scent when and where necessary – it stops the flight/escape reflex of the female.

Not surprisingly, light plays a major role in the life of butterflies. It is light that allows monarch males to see and to be bewitched by their females. However, this interest would be of no avail if the female were not put into the mood to mate. Monarchs make use of an aphrodisiac named danaidone, a substance they synthesize from specific plant alkaloids. During his courtship flight, the male monarch rubs the scent hairs on his abdomen to induce an irresistible smell that, one might say, the female antennae imbibe voraciously. The effect is, as already stated, stop and go. The reflex to flee is blocked and the willingness to copulate fueled.

Monarchs eventually acquire something like an imprinted scent memory. It has been discovered that monarch females searching for food not only react to the scent of the flowers of nutritious plants, but also to the fragrance of certain orchids – which means that they react to scents that offer them

absolutely no promise of sustenance. After further research, it has now been revealed that the scent of the orchid is similar to the signals sent out by males of a related butterfly species. This could be purely coincidental, but it could mean that in an earlier stage of evolution, monarch males also transmitted this scent frequency to entice the female, and the attraction to this scent has remained in the monarch female's genes.

The answer as to who ultimately fits best with whom can be found in the lock and key principle, which basically applies to almost all butterflies and moths and prevents cross-breeding among various species. The sclerotic, armor-like sexual organs of the monarch male must be a perfect match for the female's genitals. Anyone who has spent any time with butterfly experts – and, in particular, with moth experts – has probably heard them say something like, "If I can't identify it, then I shall have to genitalize it!" In other words, a look through the microscope at the miniscule sexual organs permits a definitive classification. This, of course, can only be done using the precision optical equipment available today. Commanding even greater attention are the discoveries made by the pioneers of butterfly and moth research in the nineteenth century. Back then, French entomologist Jean-Henri Fabre pinpointed – through keen obser-vation and many experiments – the location of the olfactory senses of the large emperor moth. But it was not until the late 1950s that Nobel Prize winner Adolf Friedrich Butenandt first isolated a sexual attractant in moths, the bomblykol of the silk moth. Chemically aroused male moths approach in characteristic, ground-level search flights for females. This is especially pronounced in the diurnal small emperor moth. The exception to the rule – he entices, she comes; he beguiles, she is willing – can be observed in the tiger moth *Estigmene acrea* and a few other species in that family. Males wishing to mate gather in a group and entice others: both males and females. The result is tantamount to moth group sex, although it is unclear what role scent plays in this equation.

Humans have been making use of the olfactory sexual dependence of moths for years, most especially against those species they do not like. Pheromone traps have a role to play in pest control. Widely distributed pheromone strips, used in the so-called disorientation method, emit such a high concentration of female scent that males lose their orientation. Either they are not able to pinpoint the target of their lust anymore, which leads to a complete failure of mating, or they land on the sticky traps from which they cannot free themselves.

148 understands the signal correctly, even though she has no experience: a member of her species flies to her as if she were a calyx and bumps her slightly in the process. *148* flies off, flees – no, appears to flee. The male follows her and, because her flight is strangely slow, he stops her without much effort. He seizes her. In the diminishing sunlight, they both spin downward, like two gliders that have collided. They find themselves on the ground, and cling together in a bed of fir needles. A little coercion from him, a little resistance from her, and it is all over.

148's "husband by chance" does something wise without knowing it – he uses the rest of the daylight to transfer sperm. The advantage of this from a male perspective is that by keeping the female occupied until twilight he keeps other male competitors away until they retreat to sleep for the night. This is no exaggeration: monarch females

148 UNDERSTANDS THE SIGNAL CORRECTLY, EVEN THOUGH SHE HAS NO EXPERIENCE

Pages 74/75: *Monarchs mating during the last third of their time in their winter quarters. The female stores the sperm implanted in her and will use it later to fertilize her eggs.*

*Monarchs use their clawed
feet to steady themselves
even on smooth surfaces.
This ability to grip is
especially advantageous
on windy days.*

tend to be polyandrous – they mate with a number of candidates, one after the other, thus ensuring access to the richest possible gene pool. His purpose is to pass on his genes exclusively, and this is only possible if he can keep the competition away.

Two days before the start of the long return flight, and two days after surviving a cold rainstorm, *148* has received – in a special storage pouch – a supply of sperm, which she will untie later, as needed. At that time, the sperm will travel through a special duct to a sperm collection sac, the *spermatheca*. As in the case of other butterflies, the eggs will not be fertilized from the sperm reservoir until just prior to the deposition of the eggs.

We as humans often have moments when we ask ourselves: "What has happened?" "Where am I?" "Where do I go from here?" Since *148* cannot herself reflect in this way, we will briefly do so on her behalf. Behind her lies a long, 2000-mile flight, across almost all of the United States: Wisconsin, Illinois, Kansas, Oklahoma, Texas and, finally, northern Mexico. She has survived a winter in the tough, high-altitude climate of central Mexico –

HE SEIZES HER. IN THE DIMINISHING SUNLIGHT, THEY BOTH SPIN DOWNWARD

only just, but survival is survival. Her task now is to bring life – in the form of several hundred eggs that are as yet unfertilized, and in the form of the sperm she carries with her – part of the way back to the Great Lakes. Just how far she gets remains to be seen. Still to be discussed, too, is the fact that she will not fly the same route she flew the previous fall, but instead will reroute the trip a few hundred miles to the east, in the direction of the Atlantic coast.

It is an aging mother that makes her way northward in the middle of March. The sperm injection has also provided her with nutrition, a little protein that

Aug.

"Birth"

Sept.

Oct.

Nov.

Dec.

Jan.

Feb.

Mar.

Departure

Apr.

Egg deposition

Death of Monarch 148

will serve as energy food for her last big exertions. The edges of her wings have fine tears, and her scaly body is worn in places. The wing skin around her identification tag is scuffed. But her ability to fly does not appear to have been impaired by the abrasion or the weight of 400 maturing eggs. It is on April 3 that a current of warm air carries *148* over the Rio Grande, several hundred miles east of the point where she crossed the border the previous autumn. A flock of shorebirds flew over the small red cloud of monarchs that floated over the shimmering expanse of the Rio Grande. No danger.

Beneficial spring rains helped to cover Texas's Edwards Plateau in a short, seasonal coat of lime green, and the slate-gray clouds on the northern horizon promised even more rain to come. Now, where but a few weeks ago a stark network of brooks and streams stood out, bushes in full flower are everywhere. Cattle country, sheep country, goat country – it is a descending line from lush to sparse to arid. The sandy traces of perpetual erosion are everywhere, erosion responsible for turning the limestone rocks into rubble, layer by layer, millennium after millennium. *148* makes her descent at ever shorter intervals. Spring flowers are so plentiful and species-rich that she does not need to search for them – she can simply drift from flower to flower with outstretched proboscis.

Every now and again *148* meets fellow monarchs – she left her traveling companions north of the Rio Grande – and other relatives at the mineral puddles where she stops to drink. A few specialized birds enjoy a bountiful feast here, but they know to steer clear of the poisonous monarchs. The nights are warm enough to keep *148* from having to spend a lot of time warming up early in the morning. Shortly after dawn, she starts on the new day as soon as the last drop of dew on her back has dried. Four

days after crossing the Rio Grande – and after spending the night well hidden – came the morning on which she did not search for nectar, but something else. With the help of the taste sensors on her legs, she tried a variety of milkweed plants. Finally, she found one with red and white flowers that seemed suitable and attached to it her first egg – an unimposing yellowish-green egg less than 0.04 inches in diameter.

The monarch motto is only one egg per leaf and never too many eggs on one milkweed plant. This ensures that things are not made too easy for egg robbers. Strategies for egg deposition are as varied as the species-rich butterflies. Hepialidae make it very easy and drop their eggs in flight. Loss is calculated and the number of eggs dropped is proportionately large. Only a few of the 44,000 eggs deposited by the Australian ghost moth, *Tirctena atripalpis*, will become moths – the freshly hatched caterpillars are decimated as they make their way out to find a source of food. But, in the majority of cases, female butterflies and moths offer pre-birth care through the selection of the right forage plants on which to deposit their eggs. In order to secure better survival chances for their offspring – in this case, to save them from dangerous travels in the caterpillar stage – it is logical not to invest a lot of time in mass egg production. And the manner in which egg clutches are arranged – singularly or in artful spirals, tiny towers or patterns – has always fascinated the butterfly and moth enthusiast, despite the fact that he cannot answer the question: "Why this way and not that?"

A few miles south of Rocksprings, Texas, *148* was attracted by a bright green circle pierced by a lighter shade of green. The hissing sound should have warned her, but monarchs do not have very good hearing. Their relatively weakly developed ability

– aided by the arteries in the forewings – to pick up acoustic vibrations is not enough for a precise warning. As she lightly fluttered to make her descent into the attractive oasis, she was met by the stream of a high-powered irrigation sprinkler. The concentrated rush of water battered her body. The wing with the code number reeled like a maple seed spinning in a pumpkin patch. And here the journey ended for *148* – a journey that, for both human observers and scientists still belongs far inside the realm of the mysterious. But perhaps *148*'s life story has an epilogue: Jonathan C. Barkley – known locally and for a good hundred-mile radius as "Pumpkin Barkley" on account of his prize-winning pumpkins – had noticed that his sprinkler was not working properly. There was something wrong with

IT IS AN AGING MOTHER THAT MAKES HER WAY NORTHWARD IN THE MIDDLE OF MARCH

the nozzle. He had had this problem last year. He trudged through the field, tested the earth for moisture with his hand and found the south-west sector definitely too dry – much too dry.

When he lifted his hand, he was startled. There was a butterfly wing stuck to it – and not just any wing. Barkley read the crumpled code number, tugged at his reading glasses and made out an e-mail address. Just a few days earlier a local radio station to which he regularly listened had run a story on "Animals of National Importance." For him, naturally, the American bald eagle – the coat of arms of the United States – had been a familiar figure since his early school years, but he was astonished to learn that the monarch butterfly had similar significance. And when he discovered the code number and address on the wing, he got in touch with

ONLY ONE EGG PER LEAF

the research program about which the professor from Kansas had been interviewed on the radio. Pumpkin Barkley made a mental note of the name: Taylor. He received a friendly answer via e-mail. And at the University of Kansas, the monarch puzzle received two new corresponding points: one in Wisconsin, just south of Milwaukee, and one in Texas, not far from Rocksprings.

Pages 82/83: Not all monarch butterflies survive the long winter weeks in the Mexican mountains. Many have been weakened by the exertions of the journey.

Page 84: On the way back to their North American home, the females deposit their eggs. They are just 0.06 inches long and scarcely detectable in the vegetation.

By butterfly standards, the demise of *148* was a happy ending. What really counts is the life that is passed on, not the individual. *148* had been able, in the previous days, to deposit a good half of her approximately 400 eggs onto milkweed leaves. And the flight plan for the return trip had been imprinted in each egg. It is a route markedly east of the original, migratory trip *148* had flown six months earlier: Texas, Arkansas, Western Missouri.

Where does this eastern route come from? Would it not be easier to follow the same route for the

Pages 87-89: *Milkweed is not demanding and thrives in any soil. All along the migratory route, it provides the monarch butterflies and their caterpillars with fresh, nourishing food.*

Mar.

Apr.

Egg

May

Jun.

Jul.

Aug.

Sep.

THE 179TH FERTILIZED BUTTERFLY EGG OF 211

outbound flight and the return trip? To date, science can provide only a tentative answer. Is it possible that it was humans who displaced the monarchs? Original summer brood centers – the nurseries of the first return-trip generation – were located in the prairie states of the Midwest: that means somewhere along the outbound route. For example, Savannah offered more than twenty species of milkweed for the caterpillar and a plethora of fruitful, nectar-filled flowers for flying insects in addition. But it did not stay that way: little by little, the plough, then the mule-drawn harvester, destroyed this butterfly paradise. And by 1910, cornfields covered the prairies.

If this explanation for the pronounced eastward turn applies, there must be something like a variable instilled into the butterfly compass system: "Warning to all monarchs! If the plant selection for caterpillars and adults is mediocre or bad, abandon the route!"

It is a variable that becomes a constant as soon as the deviation from the long-used route proves successful. But how does the course correction for the return trip become so ingrained that new generations fly the new route as though there had never been an old one? And what do the so-called California monarchs do? Butterflies west of the Rocky Mountains do not fly to Mexico to overwinter, but rather to a few chosen places in southern California. The Rocky Mountains are, perhaps, a sort of line of separation. The exact location of the border between "Californians" and "Mexicans" remains unclear.

For the experts, there is still much to do. We shall stay with the "Mexicans" and discover a milkweed sprinkled with light brown dust. This is the designated birthplace of *148a*. One day before the irrigation hose battered her, his mother, *148*, discharged this scarcely weighable load – the 179th

HE HAD A WEAPON, OR MORE SPECIFICALLY A MODEST, PROTECTIVE SHIELD

By consuming milkweed, monarch butterfly caterpillars ingest the poisons they use to ward off predators. Their warning colors mark them as inedible.

fertilized butterfly egg of 211 – a few flight hours to the south. The fact that the leaf on which *148a* was born went completely unnoticed by ichneumon flies and other enemies is probably the result of the repelling nature of the limestone powder coating the Texan wind had blown all over it. Or, perhaps, it was simply luck, or more specifically the statistical distribution of life and death. In any case, *148a* had cleared the first hurdle of his life when, after a few days of maturation, the tiny caterpillar was able to chew through the eggshell. From now on, at least, he had a weapon, or more specifically a modest, protective shield – the warning signal to potential caterpillar hunters that he is highly toxic. It is a toxicity that *148a* has first to acquire by consuming the forage plant – and its toxic cardiac glycosides, the so-called cardenolides – on which the egg once rested.

Only a few butterfly hunters can eat this poison without being harmed. But for those species that possess the necessary digestive juices, the monarch orange is not a warning, but a promise of nourishment. Such species include the black-headed grosbeak and the black-backed oriole. The grosbeaks eat the fat-rich monarch abdomen and tolerate the poison – somehow. No one knows exactly how. The oriole slits open the butterfly's body with its sharp beak and manages to lick out the contents of the thorax and abdomen. It is possible that its precision allows it to avoid the particularly poisonous parts.

Caterpillars, particularly the many non-poisonous ones, have every reason in the world to watch out for themselves. There is one thing that these relatively immobile munching machines certainly cannot do and that is to fly. So what is a plump

Mar.

Apr.

Egg

Caterpillar
stage

May

Jun.

Jul.

Aug.

Sep.

morsel to do about all the winged and the four, six and eight-legged hunters who see it as a nutritious meal? The one thing that helps is to hide.

Caterpillars that can eat extremely quickly and retreat into an inaccessible, hard-to-find spot have the greatest advantage. Several deltoid moth species do this when they wait until darkness falls to go in search of food. Numerous moth species – such as members of the Tortricidae, Pyralidae, Gelechiidae and Yponomeutidae families – actually set up defensive barricades, made of rolled up leaves or webs, on their hidden caterpillar nests to obstruct the enemy. Even better at protecting themselves are the leaf mining moths: their caterpillars tunnel into leaves. There are also caterpillars, such as the South American king's swallowtail, that pretend to be bird droppings. They are so successful that many potential predators are taken in. And if they are not, the imitator can spray a foul-smelling liquid at them from an orange-colored "yoke" around its neck as it falls. Known and loved in all of Europe, the swallowtail butterfly does much the same thing. Other impersonators take on the appearance of leaves, bark or branches. With their stiff underlayer that stands out from their bodies, some inchworm caterpillars imitate branches to perfection. This is a great help in staving off optically-oriented hunters, but those hiding teach those searching and vice versa – evolutionary biologists speak of regular "armament spirals."

THERE IS ONLY ONE SOLUTION: TO HIDE

Another effective survival strategy is the scare tactic: either the outside appearance is made "painful" or the inside is made poisonous, a fact advertised by warning colors. This technique is the monarch's silver bullet.

Monarch caterpillars are vegetarians, like almost all butterfly and moth caterpillars. But in common with all monarchs, *148a* will make one small exception. When he has finished eating his eggshell, he will eat a freshly-hatched fellow monarch that is, like him, only three-quarters of an inch in length. Although monarch females deposit only one egg per leaf, it often happens that one female after another deposits her eggs on the same forage plant if it is facing the correct migratory direction.

148a – who began his life a grayish-white, and will only later don the black-white-yellow warning colors – is in luck. Gentle spring rain washes the dust from his milkweed leaf and pleasantly softens its surface. His still tiny mandibles score the leaf, which spews forth a milky white liquid but with such force that he is in danger of choking. Over the coming days, *148a* will eat and eat and eat, and will thereby grow at a pace faster than any other member of the animal kingdom. In fourteen days he will have grown a good two inches in length. If a human baby grew at the same rate, it would weigh several tons after fourteen days.

Only the necessary molting breaks the rhythm of feeding. The new skin forms underneath the old one. But only when the new skin begins to push against the old skin and cause tightness does the caterpillar stop its continuous feeding. He tethers himself to a leaf with a thread that he has spun from a gland located under his mouth. A short time later he inflates himself so that the old skin rips open to reveal a "freshly lacquered" new chassis. The old skin is an important snack to be consumed before the caterpillar in his new coat dives back into the green leaves. Moltings are not only necessary changes in the coat of an overweight youth. With each new skin the outward appearance of the feeding caterpillar changes slightly. Some caterpillars go through dramatic changes in both color and/or shape.

Like all insects, *148a* has at his command three sets of thoracic legs. In addition to these six front legs – which are jointed and have claws at the end – there are four more pairs of legs toward the back of the body, the so-called "abdominal prolegs." These are pseudo, or fake, legs: evaginations (skin protrusions) flexible enough for the caterpillar to use them to hold on to stems and leaves. And, finally, one more pair of legs, the anal legs, is located in the hind region. The anal legs of the puss moth and related species, a group of nocturnal prominent moths, have metamorphosed into spectacular, frightening forks.

148a, meanwhile, is experiencing, for his fourth and final molting, luck in his misfortune. A thunderstorm swept off the leaf surface everything that could not be anchored with claws. And had he not firmly anchored himself for his latest coat change – the last before the final big one, the pupation – he would have disappeared into one of the dry streambeds that had filled with water within minutes. The minute the low storm clouds had blown over *148a* resumed his mandibular attack on the green leaves. He was still a feeder, but in his next life he would be a drinker.

A few days after the molting, *148a* did something he had, to date, avoided doing every day of his life. He left his plant, his source of nourishment. In an accelerated caterpillar endurance run, he covered many yards of bouldered surface with twists and turns and small thistle barriers. A beetle seemed to contemplate an attack, he even brought out is imposing mandibles for a moment, but in the face of the warning colors of his opponent, he abandoned his intentions. A yellow-flowered creosote bush stood behind a half-standing limestone slab well protected from the wind. *148a* scaled the inner layer of dead branches. He did not seem to have

Mar.

Apr.

Egg

May   Pupa
        stage

Jun.

Jul.

Aug.

Sep.

any well-defined search program – the bush was suitable because it was along his way. Using his anal prolegs, *148a* lifted himself into a small web he had already spun and hung upside down from a branch – the exit position of the so-called "suspended pupa." If butterflies were conscious of the stages in their life they would now wave goodbye to childhood as they head for youth. The caterpillar period is over. The pupa developed within the caterpillar during the last stage of caterpillar growth. What still looks like a caterpillar is only a fleshy garment containing the pupa. And this garment finally rips open at the neck and the pupa emerges.

148a wriggles, writhes and finally sheds the pupal skin, his former caterpillar form, like a body sock. What remains is the pupa. It is soft and green, and shimmers in the midday sun. And as the sun's rays penetrate deeper – by late afternoon the pupa already has a solid exterior – the chrysalis assumes a glittery, metallic quality. This is the starting point of the mystery.

For a long time, science did not talk about metamorphosis, something that had more to do with having forgotten rather than not knowing about it. Aristotle accurately described the transformation and its progression. But like so much ancient knowledge, by the Early Middle Ages in Europe the discovery of insect metamorphosis had been lost. And for centuries, the intellectual climate was not conducive to new discoveries. Certain questions just did not seem worth asking. To humans, caterpillars, the source material of metamorphosis, had nothing to do with the beautiful butterfly. Butterflies came from heaven. Caterpillars were just caterpillars – worms! If one saw too many of them, it must mean a plague was on the way –

IF BUTTERFLIES WERE CONSCIOUS OF THE STAGES IN THEIR LIFE, THEY WOULD NOW WAVE GOODBYE TO CHILDHOOD AS THEY HEAD FOR YOUTH

Within a few days, the initially opaque, green pupa becomes transparent. Many of the butterfly's features are recognizable minutes before hatching.

THE MYSTERY REMAINS

and whoever sent the plague would be cursed. Sometimes a great genius was needed to make an accurate assessment. In 1671, Francesco Redi – poet, philosopher, doctor, speaker of all languages in common use in Europe – claimed that caterpillars and maggots hatched from eggs. This was not speculation. Redi had observed it and simply trusted his eyes. At the time, it was an unusual approach, because the church still had the privilege of interpreting the world and its phenomena. Worms were vermin and, somehow, also the stuff of the devil. With his theory that live animals can live within other live animals – for example, the offspring of the ichneumon fly that live in maggots – Redi put an end to the Church's monopoly on interpretation. His assertions also provoked the scientific community of his day. Worms from eggs, animals inside animals? All that sounded dangerously like black magic. But once the origin of caterpillars had been explained – thanks to Redi and the many subsequent generations of insect researchers – the next question was quick to follow. What happens to caterpillars? Today, three and a half centuries after Redi, if you ask an expert for an explanation of metamorphosis – for example, the transformation of a pupated caterpillar into a flight-ready butterfly – you will hear words to the effect, "We don't know either. And we don't know at a very high level." In any case, butterflies and beetles totally change their form at the pupa stage. A swallowtail caterpillar is as different from its subsequent self as a flying insect after it has forced its way out of the chrysalis, as a sea cucumber is from a gazelle. In fact, what takes place inside the chrysalis is the complicated conversion of caterpillar organs into butterfly organs.

The whole thing happens in a sealed, airtight bag, so to speak. The mandibles and digestive tract are

Pages 96-100: The hatching of a butterfly is a magnificent event. The complete process does not take very long. Once it has broken through the chrysalis, the butterfly frees itself within seconds, unfolds and stretches its wings, and then hangs for a few minutes from the side of its former dwelling in order to dry its wings.

Mar.

Apr.

Egg

May

"Birth"
Monarch
148a

Jun.

Jul.

Aug.

Sep.

A FAIRYTALE TRANSFORMATION FROM CATERPILLAR TO BUTTERFLY

first broken down into a mushy mixture of cells. Adult organs develop from this apparent mess. Several, like the legs and some other organs, were formed during the caterpillar stage but most are new. Such adult organs as the wings, genitals, proboscis and faceted eyes emerge from the broken-down cells. If you feel that we have not fulfilled our mission to fully explain metamorphosis we have to confess that you are right. This is as far as present-day research has been able to go.

148a has undergone a fairytale transformation from caterpillar to butterfly and now only the unveiling process remains, a process that is perhaps comparable to giving birth in that it necessitates a great effort. 148a draws in air through tiny holes along the side of the chrysalis and inflates his body enough to slightly tear the chrysalis. For a while after that, he remains motionless in his casing, which is now transparent. For the human observer, this would be the equivalent of "taking a breather." Finally he manages to plant his legs outside the chrysalis and to widen the tear he has already made. His efforts cause the torn casing to swing back and forth. At long last, he manages to pull his wet, shimmering body free. He draws air anew, the fluid in his body begins to circulate through the veins, his wings unfold and stretch. And, finally, air replaces the hemolymph in the veins of his wings, which will need to dry out for a short time before they become functional. He clings to his crumpled chrysalis.

His first flight will be made easier by the strong midday sun. 148a does not have to learn anything. The first flap of his wings will be as perfect as the last: ease and elegance from the outset. A prerequisite for flight readiness, for both moths and butterflies, is the coordination of the forewings and hindwings – if they flapped independently of one another, no forward flight would be possible. But moths and butterflies – worldwide, there are about eight times more described moths than butterflies – solve the problem of coordination differently. While it is obviously effective for butterflies to let the hindwing pair grip underneath the forewings, both pairs of moth wings are usually coupled by bristles and spinules. The butterfly's filigree wings make possible a variety of flight styles, from fluttering at ten beats per second to highly elegant flights as they sail through the air. It is very different for most moth species. Their wings beat seventy times per second like the hummingbird hawk moth, which is often mistaken for a humming-bird as it "flies standing still" to drink from a flower. To add to the confusion, hummingbird hawk moths normally fly during daylight hours; they can be seen at dawn and dusk but rarely at night. Hummingbird hawk moths can fly at 40 miles per hour in a straight line, and, like the humming-bird, can also fly backwards.

HIS FIRST WING BEATS WILL BE AS PERFECT AS HIS LAST

148a's first flight is a forage flight. As he catches the smell of nectar on the wind, the young butterfly makes a ninety-degree turn as if by remote control, and flies over the arid Edwards Plateau, northwest of San Antonio, Texas, as if being pulled on a string. The rainstorms of the previous day have helped a thick row of carnations to flower in the limy sand. *148a* approaches the flowers, making a series of precision landings onto the lightly swaying objects. He does not roll in his proboscis as he moves from flower to flower – all the finesses of the daily life of the monarch had already been programmed into him while he was still in his chrysalis. He can do it all without practice. His actual – or perhaps we should say overriding – mission is not to consume nectar, but to cover as many miles as possible. And, for that reason, his forage flights have an underlying

Page 104/105: *Monarch butterflies do not only depend on open spaces and natural landscapes. Their journey takes them through typical American suburbs as well*

Mar.

Apr.

Egg

May

Mating

Death of
Monarch
148a

Jun.

Jul.

Aug.

Sep.

higher directive attached to them: keep on a north-easterly course.

148a shortens his morning warm-up time by lifting his wings into a V shape to allow the sunlight to reflect back and forth between them – an age-old butterfly trick. Low night temperatures are rare at this time of year in the southern United States but they send *148a* into what appear to be rather insubstantial hiding places. He spends one night in a shrubbery with little protection from specialized predators hiding in the hedgerows, and another in a rural goods depot where small rodents, which have no problem with monarch poison, are in residence. Perhaps more carefully chosen hiding places would be in order but presumably in the case of monarch migration, evolution emphasizes the survival of the masses and minimizes the importance of the fate of individuals. In any case, the laborious avoidance of predators would have done nothing to slow the flight of *148a*.

There is a now a new threat to monarch butterflies. They could soon be the victims of genetic manipulation and climate change. Scientists at the Universities of Kansas and Minnesota warn that, in coming years, monarchs could be among the first mass casualties of climate change. It is predicted that global climate change will bring much more precipitation and many more storms to those places where the Mexican *Danaus plexippus* spends the winter. This is very bad news for the monarchs, which can endure an astonishing level of dry cold, but not cold, wet storms.

There is something else that is worrying the experts: could genetically-manipulated corn, otherwise known as Bt-corn, attack the nerve center of this long-distance traveler? Scientists at the universities

Occasionally, spring nights are cool and damp. But the first rays of sunshine dry the dewdrops on the monarchs' wings.

Page 108/109: Once the monarch butterfly has been caught in the web of an orb-weaver spider, there is no escape. The spider quickly delivers its numbing bite. Afterward, it either consumes its booty immediately or stores the butterfly for lean times.

KEEP ON A NORTH-EASTERLY COURSE

Mar.

Apr.

May

Egg

Jun.

Jul. Death of
Monarch
148b

Aug.

Sep.

of Guleph, Iowa, Minnesota, Nebraska and Mary-land, as well as the Department of Agriculture, have examined what is the probability that monarchs will come into contact with Bt pollen. Their forage crops grow at the edges of extensive cornfields. Previous studies have shown that the growth of monarch caterpillars that consume the Bt pollen blown onto the leaves on which they feed is stunted. The US Environmental Protection Agency, EPA, proved in tests on open areas that when the corn is in flower, the developmental stage from caterpillar to flying insect is extended and the weight of the adult reduced. There is no expectation that the pollen from the genetically-manipulated corn will lead to a massive reduction in the monarch population – the worst expectations are a 2 per cent decrease – but there is yet another problem. The cultivation of new, herbicide-resistant corn and soy varieties and the associated agents used mean that there are fewer and fewer fields in which the caterpillar's only source of food, milkweed, can grow. Orley R. Taylor of the University of Kansas does not, therefore, concern himself only with the decaling of monarch butterflies, but also with the dispatch of packages of milkweed seeds in order to increase the number of sources of nutrition for monarch butterfly caterpillars. In a single summer he was able to install almost a thousand of these stations in private gardens, on golf courses, in state parks, and in schoolyards. The monarch butterfly enjoys a growing popularity, particularly among children. Countrywide, special "tagging events" are being arranged when both children and adults have the opportunity to decal monarch butterflies and to follow, via the internet, when and where "their" butterfly is found.

148a knows nothing of all that. Not far from the city of Hope, Arkansas, *148a* slows down. At the first sign of daylight he set off on a broad, rambling flight and even ignored the appetizing fields of flowers. A human observer would have come to the conclusion that he had lost his sense of direction. While flying over a typical US suburb – with its manicured lawns, flagpoles, barbecues and breadbox-shaped mailboxes – *148a*'s undefined flight suddenly became direct and purposeful. He was oriented by a scent signal and his number of wing beats doubled. Eventually, a line of fellow monarchs flew beneath him – and all of them were female. Like *148a*, they are butterflies of the first generation to be born on the return flight and are, like him, making the long journey to the north-east.

And it is here, on the last leg of the journey that we risk becoming sentimental. But we should ask the question, "Do butterflies have feelings? Can butterflies have butterflies in their stomach?" Does *148a* have something like a butterfly-like feeling of happiness when he finally finds a female who will float with him in the air before the two sink down into the bushes? We cannot know. But we can be sure that *148a* has fulfilled his biological duty and that, soon, a few hundred miles north of Hope, an egg will stick to a milkweed leaf and become *148b*. This egg will contain everything a monarch needs, including, of course, the information for the next leg of the journey, many hundreds of miles on from the place where the flight of *148a* came to an abrupt end.

This was a few days after the honeymoon. As he approached a lush polyanthus in full bloom, *148a* was caught in the circular web of a cross spider. The spider was hungry – *148a* did not have to endure long as a living keep-fresh meal.

148b and *148c* followed *148a*. All of them were short-lived summer generations – short-lived in comparison with the lifespan of the original mother,

148, the southern flyer, the overwinterer. Every generation lives through the four butterfly stages: egg, caterpillar, pupa, flying insect. And every butterfly attempts the long journey to the northeast. What is truly miraculous is that the flight plan is handed down from generation to generation.

Several million butterfly wing beats and two to three generations after *148a* has perished – the summer is fading – an egg adheres to a milkweed leaf at the southern tip of Wolf Lake. The cycle is complete. One more time. A new cycle begins with the hatching of another long-distance traveler. The still tiny caterpillar will develop a huge appetite and, in feasting, will acquire the species-typical poisonous protection it needs – day after day, bite by bite.

It is rather improbable that, after two transformations, she will land in the net of one of Taylor's scientific helpers before beginning the journey to Mexico. But it would be really quite extraordinary if she became *149*.

DO BUTTERFLIES HAVE FEELINGS?

Mar.

Apr.

May

Jun.

Egg

Jul.

Aug.

Death of
Monarch
148c

Sep.

Pages 112/113: *As the summer draws to a close, a new generation of monarch butterflies begins its journey from the shores of the Great Lakes.*

Pages 114/115: *Wing detail of a monarch butterfly.*

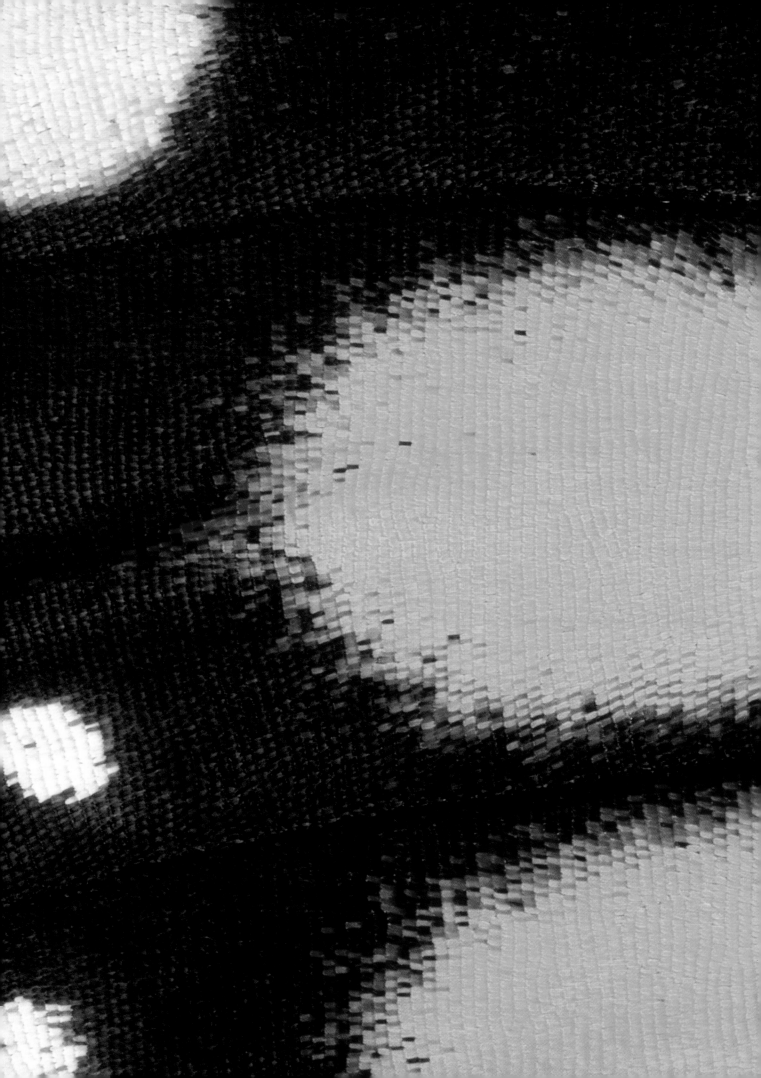

OTHER WONDERS OF THE
BUTTERFLY WORLD

EGGS, CATERPILLARS, PUPAE, BUTTERFLIES AND MOTHS

SUNNY SIDE UP Most butterflies and moths favor species-specific brood care. They deposit their eggs on plants that are edible for the hatched brood. In fact, the chosen plant is often the only possible food for the caterpillar – experts call this a "monophagous" way of life. As a rule, the eggs are secreted from a gland and affixed to a leaf. Of course, the adhesive must be weatherproof and resistant to the blazing rays of the sun and heavy rain. Right: the egg of a tropical swallowtail.

LAST-MINUTE FERTILIZATION
Not all eggs are the same – at least not those of the various butterfly and moth species. The eggs deposited in groups by the owl butterfly, *Caligo* sp., are ribbed, smooth or knobbly and some have bizarre protrusions. Even the egg form varies, ranging from round to pointed at one end. The constant here, though, is the micropyle, the fertilization opening in the egg. Shortly before the female affixes the egg to a leaf, the male sperm she has been storing penetrates the top side of the egg. The micropyle often forms a pattern at the tip of the egg. This can help experts determine the species.

GONE BANANAS For the young owl butterfly, the menu reads "egg with banana" – or, more precisely, "eggshell with banana leaf." Caterpillars often hatch simultaneously and, as a group, devour their eggshells. *Caligo* can eventually eat itself into the category of pest if mass infestation is not stopped. Perennials eaten completely bare are greatly feared by farmers in the tropics.

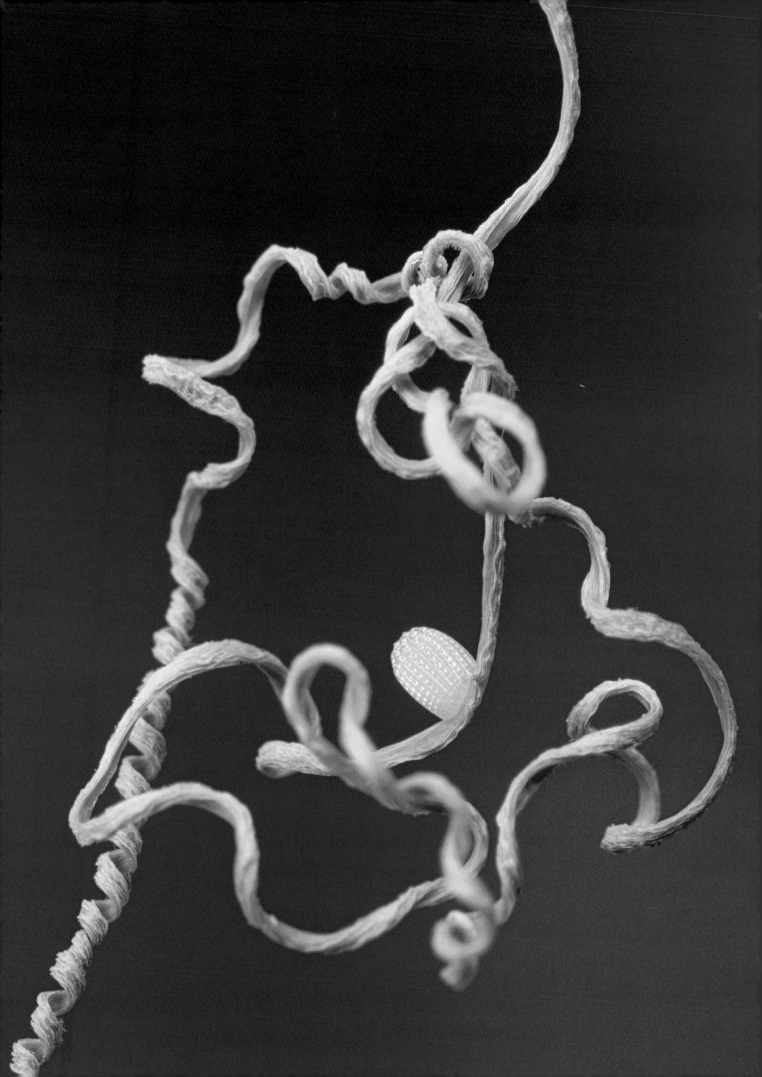

TINY BUT TOXIC Their passion is the passion plant. *Heliconius* butterfly species eat these poisonous climbing plants that grow in the tropics. Its eggs are individually placed. As with monarch butterflies, the "poison impregnation" spans the caterpillar stage, the pupa stage and adulthood. Here, too, it's eat or be eaten.

CRACKING EGGS As the egg develops, the shell changes colour. The shells of many species are translucent by the time hatching takes place. Butterfly and moth caterpillars experience the same challenge as birds when they hatch. The rather hard shell has to be broken through. Countless bird varieties use a so-called "egg tooth", a sharp protuberance on the beak, to make the work easier. Butterflies and moths, however, find it more difficult. They have to work hard with their mandibles, or biting jaws. Many species need only gnaw a large hole in the eggshell and wriggle through it. Others, such as the tropical morpho butterfly, gnaw a ring in the shell and then use the full force of their body to lift it out of the way. Once a tiny caterpillar has used up that kind of energy, it needs sustenance. For its first meal, the "newborn" – of many species, but not all – dine on the eggshell.

MAGIC TRICKS What do the defenseless creatures do when they are the desired fare of a host of caterpillar hunters? Threatening is a possibility. Warning colors, as seen in the saturnine moth *Rothschildia erycina* (page 127), are often even more effective because they are universally recognized. The fact that many poisonous – to most inedible – species wear warning colors gets around the animal kingdom. Other species can profit by wearing the same colors even though they are not poisonous. The perceived giant head of the puss moth, *Cerura vinula*, (pages 128/129) gives the impression that it is on the defensive. The "fork" on its abdomen – seen from an evolutionary standpoint it is no more than a "remodeled" pair of legs – serves to strengthen this impression. The icing on this mock-armor cake is that when threatened, the caterpillar can shoot soft, red "threads" from its tail. The fake eyes seen on the oleander hawk moth *Daphnis nerii* (page 130) serve to scare off optically oriented hunters. Colorful growths on the *Hyalophora cecropia* (page 131) are effective weapons because they are painful to the touch. The caterpillars of the death's head hawk moth *Acherontia atropos* (pages 132/133) – which is four inches long and therefore imposing – scare off the enemy just by the way they carry themselves: only a fake pose, naturally.

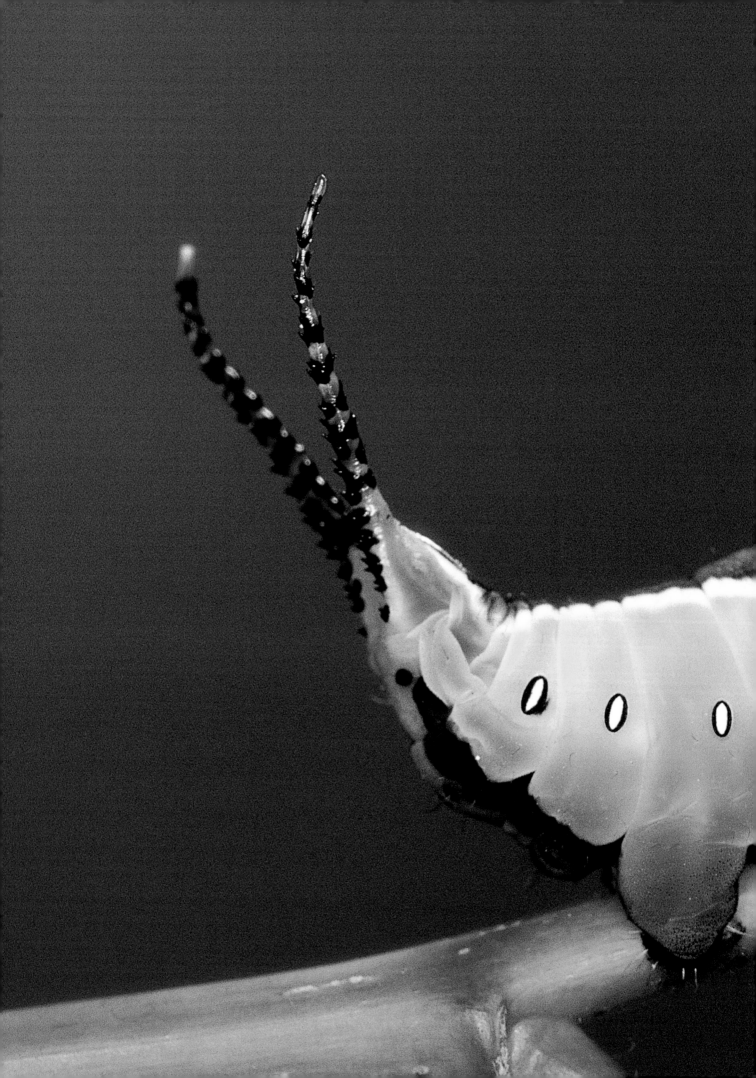

HAIRY STORIES Some caterpillars look like the fantasy concept of a whimsical designer. But even with the apparent excessive ferocity of the forms the central question is the same, "What will make me unattractive – or, better, inedible?" The thorns on the atlas moth caterpillar *Attacus atlas* (page 135) are not poisonous, but their waxy overcoat is probably quite an appetite suppressant. Conversely, the brushes sported by the festoon moth, a member of the mostly tropical *Limacodidae* family, are made up of poisonous "thorns" (pages 136/137). The skin of a species of the mainly tropical moths *Podalia orsilocha* (pages 138/139) is quite potent: even humans react strongly to touching the cuddly-looking caterpillar – pain and high fever are the usual result. These detailed images of poisonous quills (pages 140/141) are reminiscent of cacti or beds of nails.

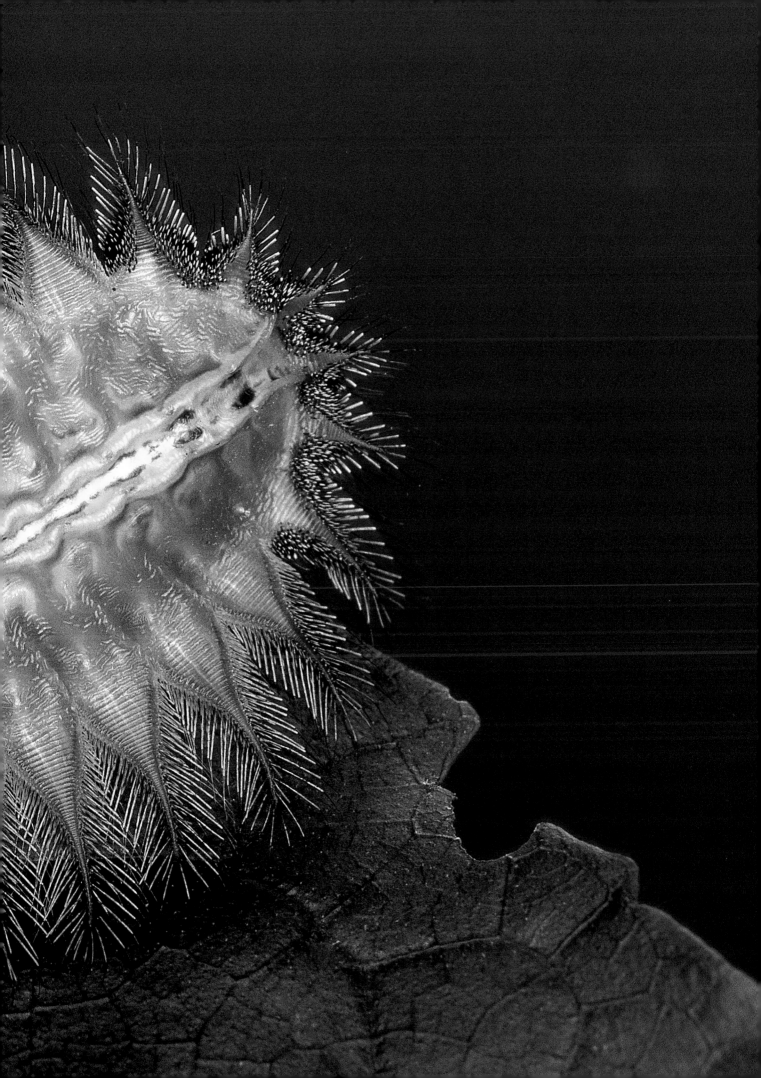

SPITEFUL TRICKS A deltoid moth caterpillar (page 142) seems to be saying, "I'm a twig". We can only assume that predators believe her and the countless other varieties of inchworm. If not, evolution would have long ago eliminated this disguise. The camouflage of the lobster moth *Stauropus fagi* (pages 144/145) seems to work on the basis of total confusion – there is nothing that looks like this on the search list of any hungry predator.

HIDE FIRST ... A swallowtail species from Costa Rica is a remarkable bird-dropping lookalike. And should this deception be unsuccessful...

... THEN FRIGHTEN ... the caterpillar releases two bright orange forks that emit a noxious smell.

IN THE BAG The abundance of pupal butterfly and moth forms may outnumber those of adults. Lepidopterologists – butterfly and moth researchers – still cannot say with certainty why that is. There is a rule in evolution that what works should not be interfered with. Chrysalises are remarkable "stay-fresh" bags, in which the transformation from caterpillar to flying insect takes place. Although they have to allow air to circulate, chrysalises must protect the tiny life form from outside influences during its transformation. Many pupae do not lie or hang unprotected in the air, but instead, in the last caterpillar stage, they make a cocoon before transforming into pupae. These allow us to see the outline of some adult parts but, through a biochemical process, the mush inside still has to be converted. It is a cocktail that even today poses numerous questions for the experts. The so-called "pupal rest" before the hatch is just one of them. *Tithoria harmonia* (page 149), *Papilio sp.* (page 150), *Dophla evelina* (page 151), *Phoebis sennae* (page 152), *Atrophaneura kotzebuea, Caligo memnon, Idea leuconoe, Athyma perius* (page 153 from top, left to right).

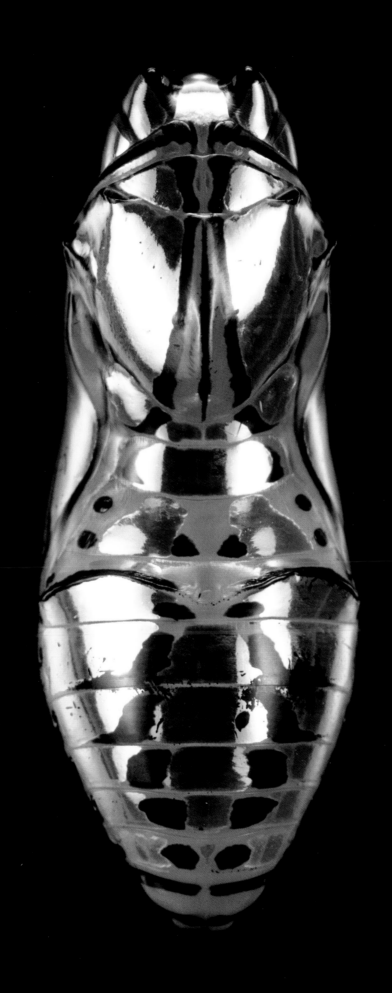

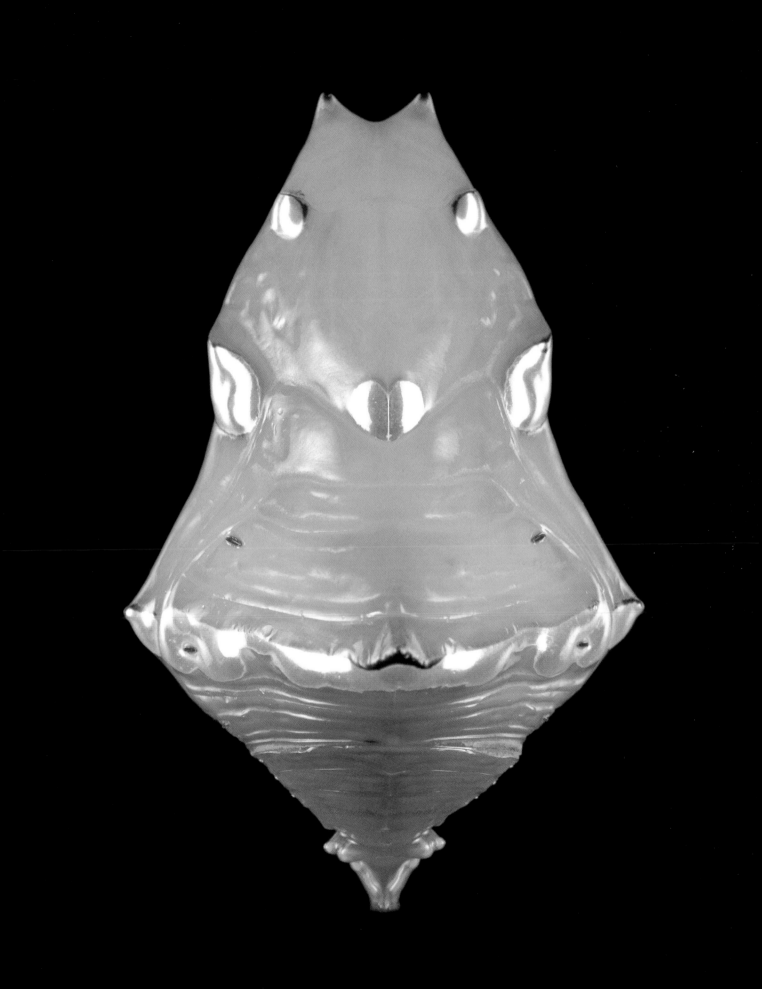

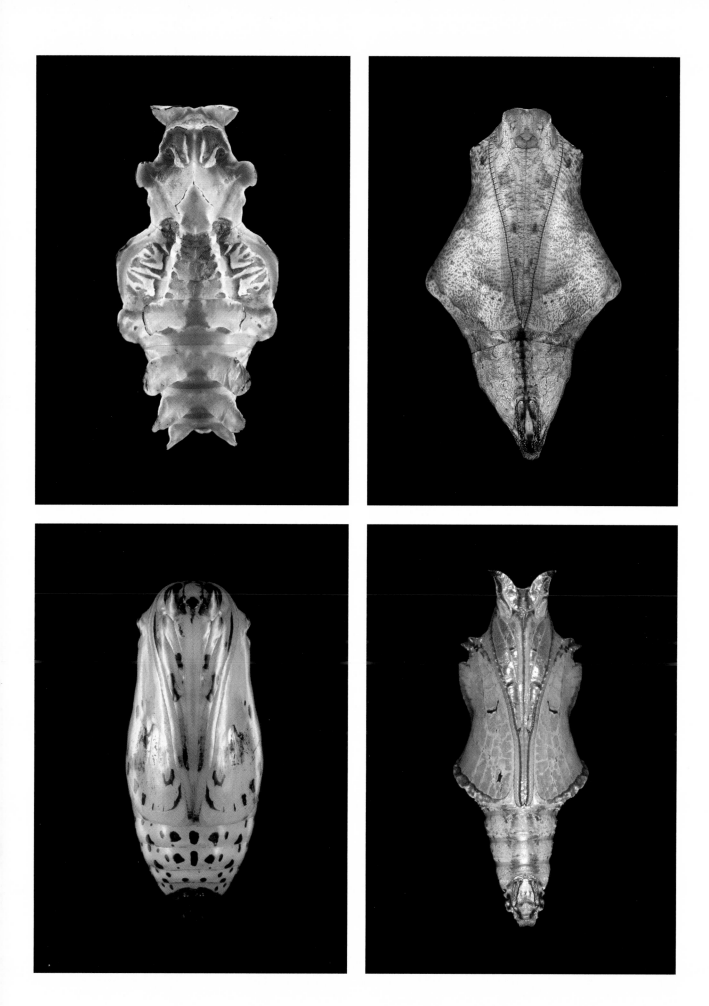

THE "TALKING" BUTTERFLY The male of the noble cracker butterfly, *Hamadryas feronia*, makes a whispering sound as it flies. Amazingly, the sound is made with only one wing. It had long been thought that it was the result of two wings being rubbed together. The clicking whispers are "sweet nothings," meant to attract females. Its "ears" can be found on the base of the forewing and not, as was thought until recently, on the antennae or head.

THE MOST TOXIC Variable burnet moths, *Zygaena carniolica*, and all other species of this family are among the most poisonous moths. They are totally inedible for most of their enemies. Their bodies contain the toxins Linamarin and Lotaustralin, which are synthesized by the "blood droplets" – another name for the moth. In addition, they can synthesize cyanide. The red dots on the dark background are, for insect-hunting birds, a potent warning sign.

THE EXTREME TRAVELER Painted lady butterflies, *Vanessa cardui*, are not winter-hardy. Every year, these flying creatures leave their homelands in North Africa and fly over the Mediterranean and the Alps to Central Europe and, in extreme cases, all the way to the Arctic Circle. But they are only summer visitors north of the Alps. Their offspring die with the first frosts although some succeed in flying back to their regions of origin – an accomplishment that has not yet been fully researched and documented.

THE "PSEUDO-STING" The hornet clearwing moth, *Sesia apiformis* (pictured below mating, and overleaf) has taken on the appearance of the well-armed large wasp. It thus profits from the fear engendered by that stinging insect (Batesian Mimicry).

THE DRUNKARD The owl butterfly, *Caligo memnon*, enjoys a banana shake – but the banana has to be overripe and fermented. The effects are obvious: after a good meal, the butterfly can no longer stand on its legs, and nor can it fly. Insect researchers often use the intoxicating effect of fruits to lure certain butterflies.

THE EARLIEST FLIER Among alpine moths, the *Lycia alpina* has a very unusual flying season. As soon as the snow begins to melt, it soars up into the skies above the mountains of Central Europe. It matches the snow and ice perfectly. A radical reversal is typical of this species: the females are unable to fly and the males have to find them.

THE BRAVEST The death's head hawk moth, *Acherontia atropos*, enters bee hives to drink the honey. The theft of food is possible only because the bees are temporarily fooled by the moth's soothing scent. But the risk is high. The worker bees are not deceived for long and discovery invokes the death penalty.

THE SURVIVOR With a life expectancy of a good eleven months, the brimstone butterfly, *Gonepteryx rhamni*, not only has the longest lifespan of all European butterflies, it is also a true winter survival artist. It keeps its bodily fluids from freezing with a frost protection agent consisting of glycerine, sorbitol and proteins. This allows it to overwinter out in the open with no protection. Even at -20° Celsius it survives.

THE SUPERLATIVE MEETING PLACE Soon after hatching, Jersey tiger moths, *Euplagia quadripunctaria*, meet up in the "valley of the butterflies" on the Greek Island of Rhodes, where they spend the hottest time of the year all crowded together. They leave in September but the next generation will meet in the valley the following year. It is estimated that there are millions of Jersey tiger moths on Rhodes each summer.

THE MASQUERADER The peppered moth, *Biston betularia*, can hardly be distinguished from the bark of the birch tree on which it rests. However, experts have pointed out that this moth is seldom to be found on a birch tree – making the value of the disguise appear somewhat dubious.

THE SMALLEST With a wingspan no more than 0.12 inches, *Ectoedemia groschkei*, a dwarf moth from Croatia, belongs to a group of the smallest moths in the world.

THE LARGEST The Southeast Asian atlas moth, *Attacus atlas* (detail above, and picture overleaf) is the largest species of moth in the world – the wing surface of the female is approximately 60 square inches. The South American white witch moth, *Thysania agrippina*, however, has a larger wingspan of almost 12 inches.

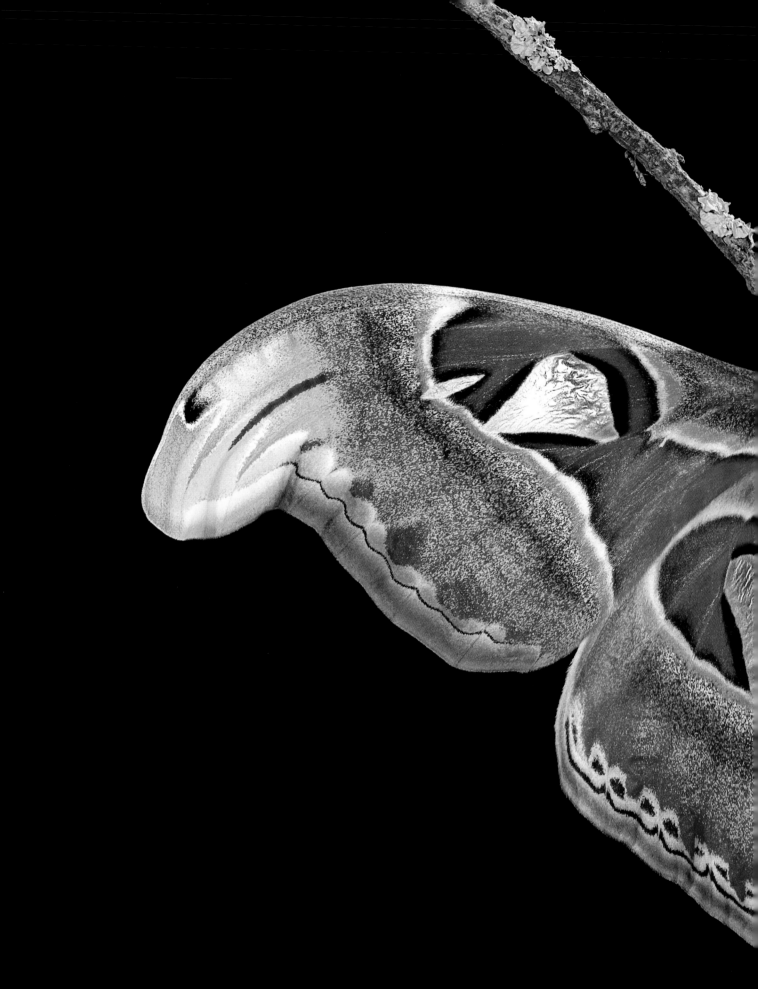

THE SUPER SNIFFER With a wingspan of up to 6 inches, the giant peacock moth, *Saturnia pyri*, is not only Europe's largest moth, but the males also have the best sense of smell. With their comb-like antennae, they can locate females within a radius of several miles.

THE DIVER China-mark caterpillars grow up under water and do not take to the air until adulthood. This brown china-mark moth pauses on the water surface for a few minutes before taking flight.

THE LONGEST The splendid Madagascar moon moth, *Argema mittrei*, is not only very large, its hindwing extensions measure up to 5 inches – a length not matched by any other species.

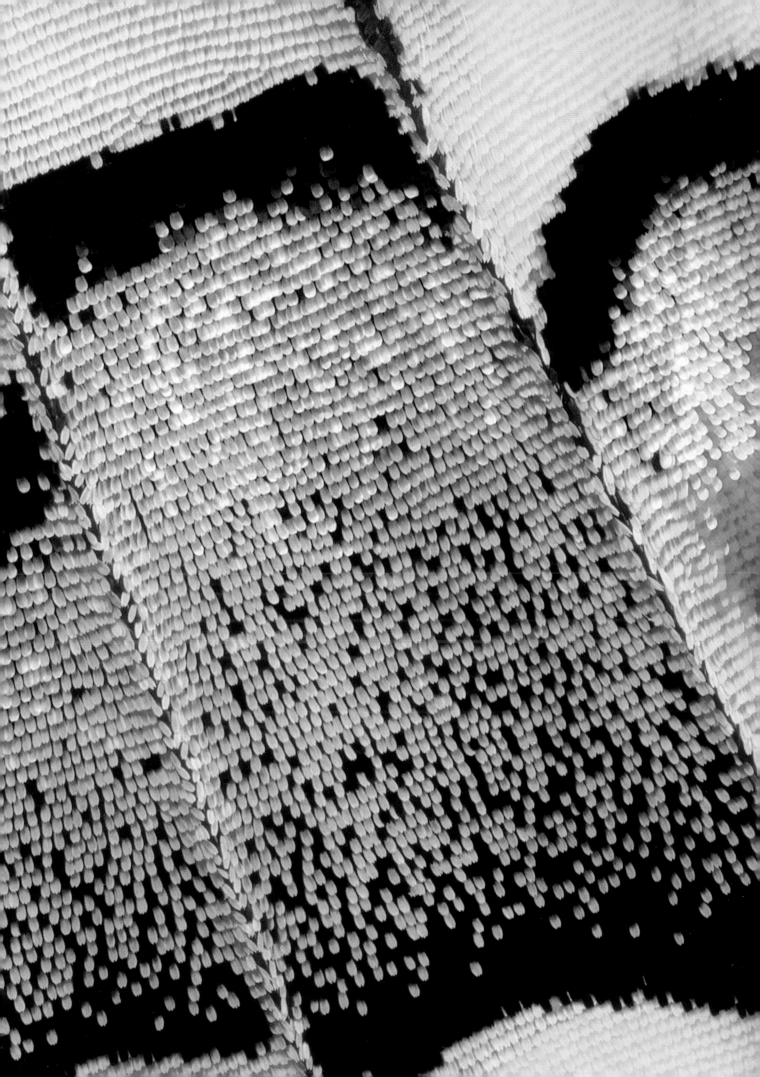

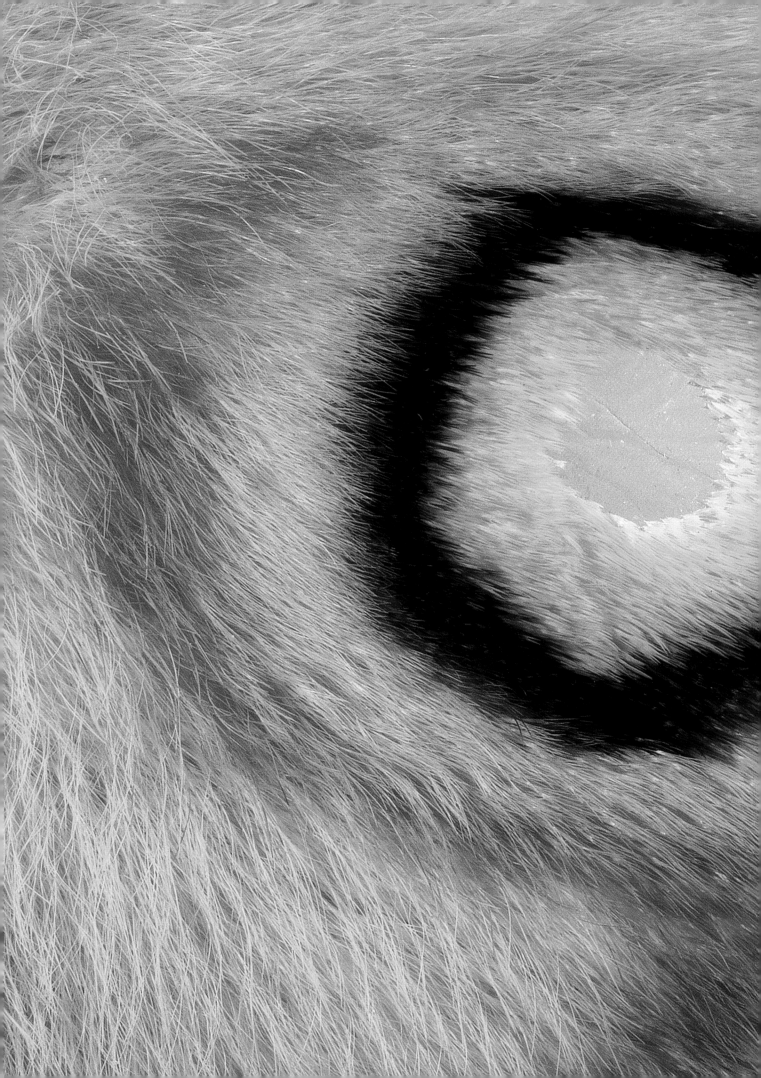

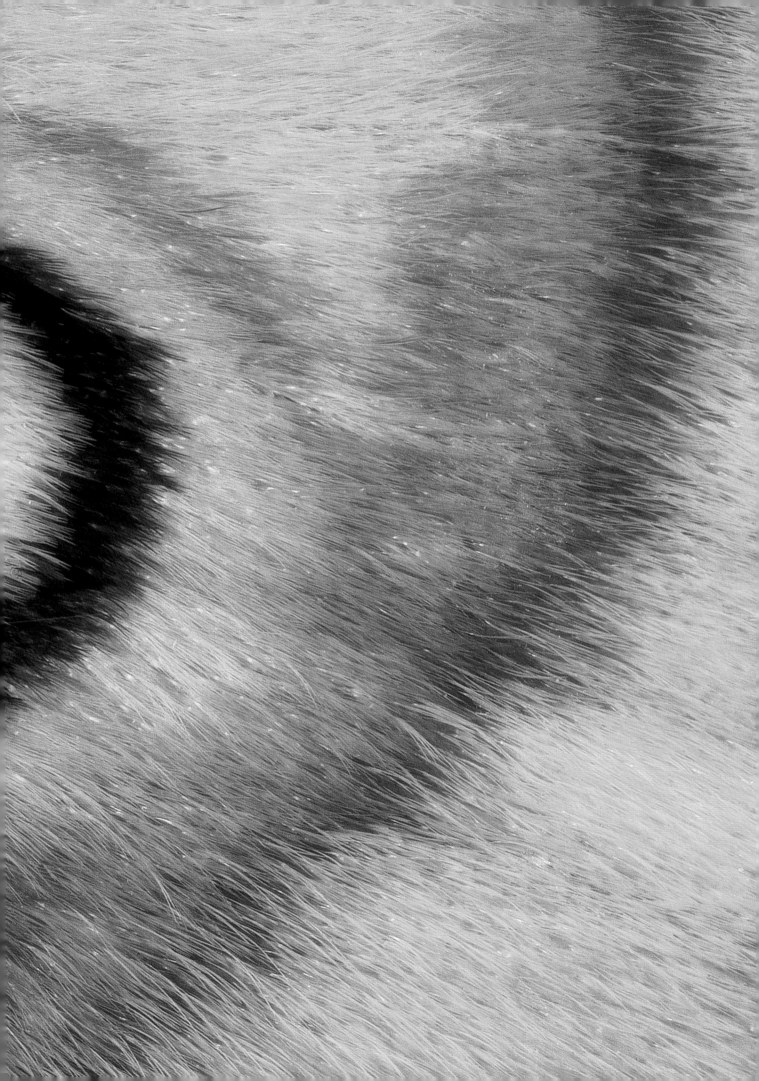

Acknowledgments

Ingo Arndt

The photographs in the book were taken almost exclusively within the past two years. Four trips abroad, more than a dozen trips within Europe and quite a number of weeks at home – where I breed a few butterfly varieties – were necessary to put together the collection of images presented here.

Such a long-term project can only be realized with the support of many people. For onsite help, I would like to extend my most heartfelt thanks to the following: Roger Blanco, Joris Brinkerhoff, Lincoln P. Brower, Hans-Martin Bürki-Spycher, Peter Buchner, John Calvert, María Marta Chavarría, John Glenndinning, Vico Gutiérrez, Erwin Hauser, Daniel Janzen, Uwe Kauz, Richard Lamb, Zdeněk Laštůvka, Kenji Nishida, Franz Pühringer, Josef Reichholf, Eduardo Rendón Salinas, Marc de Roche, Rolf Schaffroth, Eric van Schayck, George Spartalis, Wolfgang Speidel, K.J. Strookmann, Alois Trawöger, Bernhard Wenczel, Dick Walton and Louise Zemaites.

Representative for the help in the editorial department, I would especially like to thank: Ute Heek and Anett Schwarz at Frederking & Thaler; Peter Matthias Gaede, Ruth Eichhorn and Martin Meister at GEO, as well as Christiane Breustedt at GEO International. Xaver Sedlmeir and Stefan Vogt for the layout, and Karlheinz Rau for the production of the book.

Above all, I thank my wife Silke Arndt, who accompanied me on many of the trips I made for this book, ran the office in my absence, and kept in contact with our friends and family.

Claus-Peter Lieckfeld

My thanks to Karel Cerny, whose enthusiasm for and knowledge of butterflies has been such an inspiration to me. Thanks also to Veronika Straaß, who reminded me every day of Horst Stern's maxim that the love of animals must be accompanied by knowledge of them.

Peter Huemer

Numerous colleagues, not mentioned here by name, deserve my heartfelt thanks for all help great and small. I thank Helmut Höttinger for his technical copyediting and Barbara Breit for the linguistic copy-editing. My warmest thanks, however, go to my significant other, Ingrid Huemer, who, for thirty years, has endured my love of butterflies and moths – every day, without jealousy.

First published in Great Britain in 2008 by
Papadakis Publisher
An imprint of New Architecture Group Ltd.
All rights reserved

PAPADAKIS

Head office:
Kimber, Winterbourne, Berkshire RG20 8AN
Design Studio & Retail:
Studio 11 Shepherd Market, Mayfair, London W1J 7PG
Exhibition Gallery:
Monkey Island, Bray-on-Thames, Berkshire, SL6 4EE

Tel. +44 20 78 23 23 23
info@papadakis.net
www.papadakis.net

Copyright © 2008
Frederking & Thaler Verlag GmbH, München
www.frederking-thaler.de
All rights reserved

Pages 4/5: *Some days, the forest is filled with the crackling sounds emanating from the fluttering of the many monarch butterfly colonies.*

Pages 6/7: *In warm years, the few watering places in the Michoacán highlands are the only source of moisture for the monarchs.*

Pages 8/9: *Within the colonies, many tree branches are totally covered with resting butterflies.*

Pages 184/185: *Wing detail of the swallowtail butterfly,* Papilio machaon

Pages 186/187: *Wing detail of the* Morpho peleides

Pages 188/189: *Wing detail of the* Imbrasia wahlbergi

Photos: Ingo Arndt, Langen, www.ingoarndt.com
Text: Claus-Peter Lieckfeld and Peter Huemer
Captions monarch butterflies section: Ingo Arndt
Captions wonders of the butterfly world:
Claus-Peter Lieckfeld and Peter Huemer
Layout and typesetting: Wunderamt, Munich
Jacket Design: Alexandra Papadakis
Production: Verlagsservice Rau, Munich
Reproduction: Reproline Genceller, Munich
English translation © Papadakis Publisher
Senior editor English edition: Alexandra Papadakis
Editor English text: Sheila de Vallée and
Diana Moutsopoulos
English translation and copy editing: Liz Vannah
English edition typesetting: Michael Shaw

Translation, copy editing, design and typesetting coordinated by LibriSource Inc.
Printing and Binding: Tlaciarne Banská Bystrica
Printed in Slovakia

ISBN 978-1901092-929